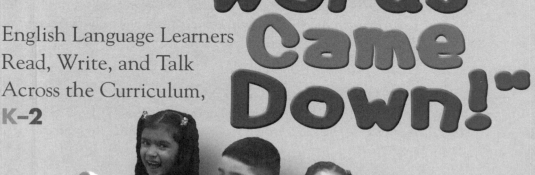

"The Words Came Down!"

English Language Learners
Read, Write, and Talk
Across the Curriculum,
K–2

Emelie Parker & Tess Pardini

Stenhouse Publishers Portland, Maine

Stenhouse Publishers
www.stenhouse.com

Credits
Pages 110–111: From *Picking Apples* by Michele Dufresne. Copyright © 2001 by Michele Dufresne. Pioneer Valley Educational Press, 31 Hidden Meadow Rd, Amherst, MA 01002. http://www.pvep.com/online. Reprinted by permission.

Library of Congress Cataloging-in-Publication Data
Parker, Emelie Lowrey, 1948–
    "The words came down!" : English language learners read, write, and talk across the curriculum, K–2 / Emelie Lowrey Parker and Tess Haysham Pardini.
        p. cm.
        Includes bibliographical references.
        ISBN-10: 1-57110-414-3
        ISBN-13: 978-1-57110-414-4
        1. English language—Study and teaching (Elementary)—Foreign speakers. 2. Language arts (Elementary) I. Pardini, Tess Haysham, 1949– II. Title.
PE1128.A2P315 2006
372.652'1044—dc22   2006045022

Cover and interior design by Martha Drury
Manufactured in the United States of America on acid-free paper
11 10 09 08 07 06 9 8 7 6 5 4 3 2 1

We dedicate this book to teachers who strive to teach in ways that will include English language learners, giving each child the gift of time to learn English.

CONTENTS

ACKNOWLEDGMENTS

This book has grown from the distillation of years of learning from each and every child we have had the opportunity to work with. Our learning has been guided and our thinking challenged by the dedicated and gifted teachers we have worked with over the years. We should give a special mention to Kent Buckley-Ess, Kathleen Fay, Suzanne Whaley, Dottie Fowler, and Noel Naylor. We have been privileged to work for two extremely committed and knowledgeable principals at Bailey's Elementary School, Carol Franz and Jean Frey. With their professional drive, these educators have lured, coaxed, encouraged, and sometimes pushed us into building communities of learners, rethinking our approach to curriculum development, instruction, and assessment. They have challenged us to keep our focus on the students and learning.

We would like to thank our colleagues who read parts of our manuscript and gave us their helpful insights: Michelle Bouchier Gale, Nora Brent, Mary Anne Buckley, Kent Buckley-Ess, Kathleen Fay, Melissa Fleischer, Carol Franz, Lynda Gill, Judy Heard, Leisha Lawrence, Lauren Nye, Melanie Rick, Lynn Riggs, Jessica Sebag, and our teams.

We must also acknowledge the gracious encouragement and thoughtful input we received from Cathy Mere and Bonnie Baer-Simahk.

Perhaps we should mention here a few educators whose work has influenced our thinking over the years: Ralph Fletcher, JoAnn Portalupi, Marie Clay, Donald Graves, Lucy Calkins, Ellin Keene, Suzanne Zimmerman, Debbie Miller, Regie Routman, Stephanie Harvey, Irene Fountas, Gay Sue Pinnell, Andrea McCarrier, Walter Secada, Lucy West, and Marilyn Burns.

Without Philippa Stratton's foresight, this book would not have unfolded. We are grateful for her trust in us, her understanding, and her never-failing support for two novice authors.

Emelie Parker and Tess Pardini

I am deeply grateful to Mum and Dad, who instinctively understood about curiosity and hands-on learning, and to Steve, my brother and learning partner in the one big field trip of our growing up together. I remember my godmother whose passion for teaching the hardest to teach inspired me. A life of travels with my husband Ed has expanded my cultural horizons. My children Eleanor and Eric have always reminded me of the wonder in the world. And I cannot imagine life without my own community of learners, my dearest friends, with whom I laugh, struggle, learn, and continue to grow. Finally, I must thank Emelie, who asked me to go on this journey with her and created the ultimate collaborative experience.

Tess

I have a thankful heart for Mama, who prayed with me before I left for school and played with me when I got home. From my mother I learned that learning did not have to be done alone and could be fun. I'm thankful for Dad, who, as editor of a daily newspaper, taught me that powerful writing is writing that is truthful. Thank you brothers Mark, Bill, Erik, and Perrin and daughters Marie, Helen, and Myra for teaching me we all are created differently. From you I learned we all learn in different ways. I'm thankful for my husband Wood, who affirms me by honoring my teaching. Hugs and thanks to my grandchildren, Emelie, Travis, Mark, Kristen, Jonathan, and Parker, who tolerate my teachable moments. A special thanks to my reflective colleagues who have challenged me always with questions such as, "How is this best for each learner?" I'm thankful for my small group and friends who have prayed with me and for me. I am thankful that all these people have taught me that surrounded by unconditional love and focused attention, we learn, we grow, and our service to others is multiplied.

From the day Tess agreed to join me in this writing endeavor, we have kept you, our audience, first in our thoughts. It has been a great privilege to work with Tess to create a book with one heart and one mind. Thank you, readers, for spending your time with us.

Emelie

Foundations

1

OUR SCHOOL

Features of Effective Programs for L2 [ELL] Learners

- *High expectations are held for L2 students.*
- *Language and subject matter are integrated.*
- *Concept development in the L1 [first or home language] is supported.*
- *Comprehensive staff development for all faculty and staff is provided.*
- *The entire school environment supports L2 learners.*
- *Active support from school leaders.*

Samway and McKeon, *Myths and Realities*

If you were to visit Bailey's Elementary School for the Arts and Sciences, you would immediately be struck by the vibrancy within its walls. The walls are colorful extensions of the classrooms; the administrators are caring, knowledgeable, and engaged; the teachers are friendly, enthusiastic, and flexible; and the students, well, they are amazing!

Bailey's serves about 900 students in Fairfax County, Virginia. About 200 students arrive by bus or by car from outside our boundaries and attend our schoolwide magnet program, drawn by the rich variety of resources. The magnet program was developed many years ago in order to attract English-speaking role models to our school, and it continues to evolve as resources and needs change.

Nevertheless, most of our students live within our boundaries. The neighborhood encompasses families who live in expensive single-family homes and hold stable, professional jobs. It also includes immigrant families with strong work and education ethics. However, 75 percent of the school population receives free or reduced lunch, and the majority of these children live in overcrowded apartments nearby.

There are children who come from families where one or both parents are illiterate in their own language. Some parents are unemployed or work sporadically as day laborers, while others hold down two, or even three, jobs. Some families share apartments with extended family members or rent rooms to others in order to share household expenses. Many of these families are also contributing to the support of relatives in their native countries.

The children attending Bailey's come from over forty countries and speak twenty languages. Some have recently arrived in the U.S. and may never have attended school in their native countries. Others speak no English but are literate in their native language. Others were born here but did not speak English until they started school. Some have lived here long enough to have developed good oral English and act as interpreters for their parents.

Over the years, people have repeatedly asked questions like, "How do you teach at a school with so many ESOL students? Can you speak all those languages? What do you do when the children can't understand you?" In this book we will explain how we have learned with our colleagues past and present to meet this challenge. We will present the philosophy of our school and discuss how we as a community of learners try to figure out what each child needs.

We don't remember life before Bailey's, we've been here so long. Between us we have taught at Bailey's for over thirty-five years. We have both taught kindergarten as well as first and second grade and worked as writing resource teachers. Emelie is a math resource teacher and Tess, a Reading Recovery teacher. Our hearts, however, will always be in the classroom.

We have known many students who have taught us so much about language acquisition, inclusion, accepting approximations, and celebrating even the smallest learning. We have grown with some of the most dedicated, inquiring, and gifted colleagues who challenge our thinking. Our administrators have traveled with us into the unknown, provided leadership when needed, and trusted us to charge ahead when we felt it was necessary. Our division always meets head on the latest challenges in education, deciding how to integrate these challenges into support for our students and their families. In order to do this, each has provided us with some outstanding staff development opportunities. Therefore, although the challenges of our population have been great, we have not had to face them alone.

However, we know that there are teachers and administrators across America who are seeing the makeup of their populations change rapidly. We hope that, by sharing our beliefs and our own learning, we can help these educators support all students, whatever their backgrounds, with joy and enthusiasm.

Over the years of teaching second language learners we have had the guidance and expertise of Kent Buckley-Ess, our English for students of other languages (ESOL) instructor extraordinaire. He has been our mentor, showing us how to put into practice the latest research in language acquisition. Kent has helped us to realize that what benefits all students benefits our English language learners (ELLs). This mind-set of implementing the best practices that accommodate all students prevails across the school. Thus, all teachers at Bailey's consider themselves ESOL teachers.

Kent now teaches fifth-grade ESOL students for half the day and heads up the ESOL team. During the other part of his day, he acts as the coordinator and instructor of an innovative ESOL resource program he developed within our division using Bailey's as a lab school. Teaching teams from other schools visit Bailey's for the day to see how teachers differentiate instruction for ELL students within the classroom setting. Teams might include ESOL teachers, their general education coteachers, and often administrators. This past year Kent scheduled visits for approximately 200 teachers. The visiting teachers specify what types of classrooms they want to visit and what they want to see happening in these classrooms (for example, fourth-grade writing instruction in an ESOL pull-out setting, second-grade guided reading in an inclusion classroom setting). Kent schedules a rotation of teachers for them to observe. Later he meets up with the visitors for a working lunch, and together they spend the afternoon discussing their visit and their own site-specific concerns.

Most often visitors ask to see how classroom teachers differentiate and present material to a class that includes ELLs when the ESOL teacher is not present. This allows them to see differentiation that is all-encompassing.

They are also interested in seeing examples of coteaching and looking at our Writing Lab. (This setting provides small-group support for fifth-grade students whose oral language is quite fluent but whose writing is not meeting grade-level expectations.)

Visiting teachers all comment that the afternoon's discussion with Kent is what allows them to improve the way they deliver instruction based on the needs of their own students in their own communities. Kent feels part of his role is to help teachers see what they are already doing that will benefit the ESOL students and where they can make some simple adjustments to make instruction more meaningful and beneficial in many ways. For example, Kent points out, "The agenda is already up, so one can just add some pictures to point to as the day progresses." Other small adjustments he suggests are "purposeful pairing of students in small groups or partners; use of centers for additional language time; and lots of time to talk, pauses to think, and lots of wait time."

We have asked Kent to summarize the evolution of the ESOL program at Bailey's.

Eighteen years ago we were just starting to bring ESOL students back to their neighborhood schools. Previously they attended center schools—centrally located schools that received all ELL students from neighboring elementary schools. Of course, the immigrant population was just beginning to mushroom at this end of the county then, and it had not yet impacted the western end of the county at all, as it has today. Now we are fortunate to provide educational opportunities to most ELL students in their neighborhood elementary school.

Fifteen years ago, we tried to service our students through pull-out support, but that wasn't as successful as we wanted it to be. There always seemed to be scheduling concerns that arose when ELL students were pulled out for language instruction during other content area time, such as math, science, or social studies. And, it was no longer practical as our numbers continued to grow.

Certain events have caused us to develop in the way that we have. Some have been school related, some have been divisionwide changes, and some have been statewide expectations. Most recently, nationwide demands are forcing us to examine how we can balance the time our ELLs need to acquire language with the pressure to accelerate their learning placed upon us by the No Child Left Behind Act.

But traditionally at Bailey's, grade-level teams have decided how they could use their ESOL positions best in order to meet student needs at that grade level. Our numbers of ELLs ensure that there is at least one ESOL teacher at every grade level.

In kindergarten and first grade, where the majority of our ELLs have only a little, or limited, English proficiency, we choose to use our ESOL position as a regular classroom teacher. This helps to keep class size down and enables the ELLs to spend all day with English speaking role models, as well as other students who speak a range of levels of English.

Last year second grade decided to pull out only small groups of students who are at the preproductive and early productive stages of English acquisition for an hour a day. The ESOL teachers "push in" to the classrooms at other times of the day to support the ELLs. Coteaching with the classroom teachers enables them to provide an inclusion model of delivery of instruction.

The third-, fourth-, and fifth-grade teams have also chosen to move to a model of limited pull-out instruction and increased inclusion support in recent years. These changes in the method of delivery of instruction have come about as our understanding of language acquisition is evolving across our division and within our own building.

The following terms are common throughout the world to describe the general stages of language acquisition, regardless of native language spoken by the ELL.

Preproduction: The students are storehousing the new language. They might point, nod, or gesture. (Length of time = ten hours to six months; Language acquisition = 500 receptive words; often referred to as the "silent stage.")

Early production: The students internalize more language and might communicate through yes/no answers or single words, or repeat a patterned response, such as, "Good morning. My name is . . . ." (Six more months; 1000 receptive active words.)

Speech emergence: The students begin to use phrases or simple sentences. Students are becoming comfortable in using social language within the classroom setting. (One more year; 3000 active words.)

Intermediate fluency: Students continue to gain and use social language skills. They also are learning and beginning to use specific vocabulary and concepts related to academic language. (Again, one more year; 6000 active words.)

Continued language development: The students are engaged in classroom activities. They are refining the challenging academic language and concepts needed in content courses. (Five to ten years; content area vocabulary.)

Throughout each stage, teachers are constantly gauging when to provide more or less support for comprehension, academic language, or cultural information.

The ways students communicate in each stage are the same ways teachers must assess the ELL students. A preproductive first grader, for example, might be able to point to the continents on a map during class time. When it comes time for assessment, she cannot be held responsible for saying the name of a continent from memory. A more appropriate assessment would be to identify the continents by pointing to them. If she can name one or two, that is fine. Assuming that the same maps were used for instruction and review, this type of assessment would be appropriate for a preproduction stage ELL and would give the teacher meaningful feedback on both language and content material.

Researcher Jim Cummins coined the terms BICS and CALP to describe the two distinct areas of language acquisition that students encounter. Basic Interpersonal Communication Skills refers to the everyday language needed in order to communicate with those around us and get through our day. We have learned that it is more effective to set up learning experiences within the classroom that allow these essential conversations to happen naturally. A pull-out class that emphasizes the formal rehearsal of language will not provide the social interaction necessary to develop such everyday language.

The focus of teaching English as a second language, both in our division and on the national front, has moved beyond just BICS to include CALP, Cognitive Academic Language Proficiency. This refers to content academic language that might have fewer, if any, concrete references. It is more difficult for an ELL to express and to understand. Additionally, content vocabulary and concepts are often difficult for teachers to communicate to ELLs (for example, such terms as *natural resource* and *prediction*). Content academic language includes textbook language, lecture, literary conventions, nonverbal communication, content vocabulary, connective language, cultural understanding, and humor. It takes from five to ten years for a student to become proficient in using such language. We must explicitly teach this language as it is not necessarily absorbed or implicitly understood.

Connective discourse allows the children to practice more formal language that will benefit them academically and in interpersonal relationships of a more formal nature, such as a written report, an oral presentation, or a job interview. We must teach and model academic language structures and hold students accountable for using these language structures by building them into our class discussions so that students may practice. For example, we should expect a student to say, "I agree with Lupita's idea" rather than saying, "Me too." Having said this, it is necessary to realize that our expectations for every student are based on our knowledge about that student's current level of English acquisition. If you are interested in exploring cognitive language further, we suggest reading Kevin Feldman and Kate Kinsella's work entitled "Narrowing the Language Gap: The Case for Explicit Vocabulary Instruction" (Kinsella and Feldman 2003).

In the following chapters, we describe how we teach both basic and cognitive language to students during our day. We do not have a specific chapter on oral language because, as with everything, we are constantly assessing its development. We have allowed students to express their learning in alternative ways. Rather than dealing with oral language or assessment as separate issues we have interwoven them throughout the book just as we interweave them into every moment of every day.

We know that sooner or later all our ELLs will experience national, state, and division assessments. The Bailey's faculty continues an ongoing discussion of how to best prepare our students for such tests and help them develop a command of the kinds of academic language they will need to control in order to comprehend these tests. At the primary grades we consciously teach words in the context of the day that children will find embedded in their state standards testing. For example, we use words such as *chart, table, above, nearest.* And we listen carefully to our students so we can provide them with the language they need in order to make meaning. So when Kaylin says, "I see the sir," we know she sees the man. We can model the word *man* for her in our conversations until it becomes part of her vocabulary. When Saul says *bug* for *bud* and *mug* for *mud,* we know he sees the buds and mud on our nature walk and continue the conversation with him to increase his scientific learning.

In this book we share stories of other children like Kaylin and Saul, stories of ELLs and our staff who teach them. Providing a window into our classroom communities allows us to share some insights into meeting the challenges of working with English language learners across the curriculum. It is so important that we as educators take risks, enjoy the journey, and allow plenty of time to listen and talk to both students and colleagues.

2

BUILDING COMMUNITY

One of the most astonishing bits of advice, gleefully endorsed by many students, was the students' desire to speak English in fun, informal contexts: "We need to play in English, not just speak in English in school." . . . When students "play in English" in addition to learning the formal English of the classroom, they begin to acquire the casual informality that enriches any language and gives the speaker confidence.

Douglas R. Reeves, "If I Said Something Wrong, I Was Afraid."

11

A Community of Learners

Emelie's lesson plan for the hour after lunch and recess on March 17, St. Patrick's Day, was for children to self-select learning centers. While they were busy learning through play, Emelie would pull out individual students or small groups for additional language arts or math instruction.

When the children came in from recess, where they had spent their time frantically looking through the leaves for a leprechaun, they eagerly made their decisions about what they wanted to do for the next hour. Emelie's plan was to look at her list of children who needed extra help. She would then work with any child who was having a hard time settling down. She gathered her clipboard, magnetic letters, tub of counters, dry-erase board and glanced up to see whom she should call to work with first. She started watching the children, noticing the oral language and both the academic and social learning that was going on in the room. The more she noticed, the more she did not want to interrupt this community of learners.

In the science laboratory designed by the children were Sarah, Zayd, and Bruce Lee. They had spread a towel on the sand/water table and pulled out numerous sizes and shapes of beakers. The three were continuously chatting about what they observed as they blew bubbles, measured and transferred water from one container to another, cleaned up their spills, and discovered they could use straws to suck up water and hold it before releasing it into a new container.

Other children were huddled around computers, working on new science and language-arts software that a colleague had dropped off during lunch. Because it was new software for all of them, Emelie kept waiting for them to ask her a question. They never once asked for help but preferred to explore the unknown together. She was especially interested in what was going on at one computer where a Spanish speaker, an Urdu speaker, and a Chinese speaker were successfully navigating a Spanish science CD together. Others were involved in listening and following the directions to decipher how to play the new games on the computer on their own. They listened to the computer and to each other as they explained their attempts. They were patient with mistakes and rejoiced in successes.

A group of six children started stirring green pudding made from leprechaun dust (pistachio pudding) and leprechaun juice (milk) in a black cast-iron skillet. They were pretending to pour from a large brass pitcher. The leftover broccoli from the class's leprechaun feast became a vegetable tray. Around the broccoli, Nancy artfully arranged felt circles with stars on top. They pulled out math manipulatives to use as elaborately decorated cookies and cakes. Chairs turned into seats for a van. A lid from a canister became a steering wheel. Gabriel became the father, Kelsi the mother; all others became aunts, uncles, and cousins. They all carried gifts and foods carefully in their laps or stored under seats. Kelsi scooted over to her back-pack and pulled out a baby doll, which she fastened in an upside-down stool for a car seat, and off they drove to the baby's birthday party. Planning the menu and setting up the van had taken so much talk. They had even delivered a written party invitation to their friends in the science laboratory. The friends declined. Those packed into the van giggled and waved goodbye as they drove off to the party.

At another table, Ms. Kim and several children sponge painted on construction paper to make petals like the real ones we had seen the day before on our nature walk. They referred to nonfiction texts to make their art accurate. The children were involved in casual conversation rich with science vocabulary as they worked with the instructional assistant and were learning words such as *petals, stem, bush, leaves, crocus,* and *pussy willow.* They proudly cut out and glued their art to the "Looking for Spring" mural in the hallway. They were working on writing and spelling as they carefully labeled these new additions and chatted about the time line depicting spring. Students added words on the mural helping them learn *mud, ants, petals, roots, leaves, sprouts,* and the difference between *bud* and *bug.*

Emelie listened in wonder as children who came into the room in September with little or no English took part in advanced negotiations as they solved problems during cooperative learning and play. They were learning from each other and discovering together as they played. The children had not learned the color words or object words through drill. They had learned the words as well as language structures through listening, reading, writing, and using language in meaningful and purposeful ways. They were becoming English speakers who could take risks with social, academic, and content language.

Emelie never did call anyone to work with individually that hour. She was sorry they had to stop such rich language learning, clean up, and go to PE.

This wonderful afternoon with a little community of learners happened because of serious planning before school opened and throughout the year. It takes more than just thinking about building community to end up with a community of learners who can work, play, and learn together. It takes lots of focused work by children, teachers, and even the whole school community to build bridges to cross the language, culture, and age barriers.

Children entering school for the first time bring with them such a wide range of experiences. It is necessary for them to mesh their early life experiences with the expectations required by the very different culture of school. There are social expectations placed upon them for which they might be ill prepared. Not everyone knows how to share, how to take turns, how to move safely in a crowded space, how to work or play together, or how to respect the space, thoughts, or work of others. Dr. Marie Clay has written extensively on "opening literacy doors" and believes "schools must provide bridges for children to cross into the school situation, *allowing children to bring what they already know how to do to bear on the classroom tasks.* The challenge for the school is to realize the learning potential that exists in every child" (1998).

Children need to develop a new vocabulary based on the functions of school: words such as *line-leader, cafeteria hostess, custodian, buddy reading, investigate,* and many other new words and concepts. They have to transfer an oral language code to a written code that has certain inflexible rules, such as those of directionality. They must learn to apply their rapidly increasing receptive language to oral and written language.

Anyone who teaches primary grades knows how much social and cultural learning occurs in a classroom during September. How much more difficult it must be for a child who speaks little or no English to get through these first days and to start feeling like a contributing member of the school and classroom community. There are many ways schools can support these young English language learners to insure they are all integral members of the community.

Before meeting the children, it is important for teachers to spend time becoming familiar with the social customs of the families who come to their school. "Little" things can cause a child either to feel ill at ease or to feel welcomed into the community. We need to learn the correct spelling and pronunciation of a child's name and practice it. (We have learned that you cannot always assume the gender of the child based on clothing, haircut, or the name.) We need to learn what country his or her family is from, the language they speak, and the level of literacy in the home. It is also helpful to know other social and cultural customs: some cultures do not touch children on the head, and in others, children are taught not to meet an adult's eyes; some families teach children to be dependent on their parents and others independent; some children are encouraged to speak and others to be silent.

We care so deeply about these young students as they struggle to navigate uncharted waters in this new, out-of-the-ordinary environment with its different language. There are two big areas where teachers can support these children. They are areas that build community for the whole class: the physical environment and the social and emotional environment.

Physical Environment

As teachers, we thoughtfully design a physical environment that contributes to the development of an inclusive community, one that is safe, secure, and supportive for the young learner. We spend a great deal of time sketching out our rooms, shoving furniture around, and finding the perfect placement for every center, every piece of equipment and furniture. We are thinking about the individuals who will inhabit and shape this space into a community. We design the space for interplay between each individual and the group. Let us look at how some specific areas help second language learners as they become active participants in their community.

Fostering Security and Success for All

We design our classrooms to take children who speak a variety of different languages to the place where they can play and learn with a shared common language of English. We think and talk a great deal with colleagues and walk through each other's rooms to get ideas about how to set up our own rooms and create safe, secure environments for learning. We arrange furniture so children can socialize in small groups. We want them to mimic behaviors of others and listen to the conversation around them. Interaction in small groups provides a safe environment for early risk taking with language.

We arrange all the supplies children might need throughout the day so children will be able to access them even without having the language to name them or ask for them. Our goal is to build a classroom community where every child is successful and is developing independence. For example, children who do not know the word for scissors need to see them and be able to reach them.

We plan for routines and procedures that will build respect and acceptance as well as security and success, for example, many small-group opportunities for guided practice and a circle time that honors each child's attempts at contributing. We believe in talk all day so we design rooms conducive to talk yet comfortable for silence. In order for children to take a risk and utter their first word of English, they must feel safe and secure. A child's first English word often comes when lining up to go to recess. Beginning English speakers will call out, "He cut!" These English language learners have learned that in their classroom community the routines of lining up pertain to everyone. The more thoughtful consideration we put into our learning environment, the deeper the feeling of community will be for the students. The safer children feel, the more risks they will take and the quicker they will start to acquire knowledge and language.

A Welcoming Meeting Place for Conversation

The heart of the room is the meeting area. It must be large enough for all children to gather comfortably on the floor for conversation, reading, and singing. In this space, children will share experiences through books, conversations, meetings, and shared instruction that will build community.

We are reluctant to sing solo in an adult group! However, both of us will take a risk and sing out with joy when someone beside us or behind us has a lovely voice. Those voices give us confidence and keep us on pitch. Young nonreaders or new English speakers can experience this same feeling in a well-designed meeting area. Children attempting to speak a new language will tentatively join in choral rereading of poems and Big Books if children surrounding them are reading. Soon they will be confident and joyful participants. A solid community makes everyone feel a "part of the choir."

A teacher chair or rocking chair, an easel, dry-erase board, markers, and stacks of books are the starters for this area. A teacher must always be ready to sketch a quick picture or grab a book to find a picture to illustrate a point. As the year develops, this meeting area will take on the personality of the class with student-generated charts, favorite books, children's art, lists of questions, and colorful clutter. This space is the meeting area for whole-group math, science, social studies, as well as read-aloud, writing workshop mini-lessons, and writing workshop sharing. It is the morning meeting area, class meeting area, and dance floor.

A Library That Meets the Needs and Interests of All Learners

An extension of the meeting area is the library space. We display an ever-changing selection of books face out as an invitation to all. In addition, children can browse through baskets labeled with a variety of genres, topics, and authors. Many of our ELLs are from homes with few, if any, books. We surround our students with hundreds of books and want them to learn to pick up a book and read for pleasure and information. Looking at books should be both a social and an independent activity for them. We know that the lively social interaction between children and books will help develop social and academic language. We also know that one of the best ways to develop community is to have a shared experience.

To develop a love of reading for pleasure and information, teachers read books to start the day; to begin reading, writing, math, science, and social studies lessons; and to bring closure to the day. ELLs need the illustrations to make connections with their prior knowledge, the instruction, and the oral language they hear. They need the books to show us what they know. They eagerly point to pictures to show us things they like or that interest them.

Children learn to choose from a variety of genres and reading levels in their classroom library, such as nonfiction, current unit-of-study books, math

Figure 2.1 Sorting these books will be an ongoing task for Shannon Blaney's class.

books, ABC books, and series books. They are taught from the beginning how to respect the books and where to return them. The library is set up for buddy reading and conversation. Students are delighted to see books that mirror their cultures, experiences, and languages. These shared experiences with many books help bind children together in community.

Teachers encourage book browsing and model enjoying books. We demonstrate how to have conversations while browsing through books. Children learn from the beginning that reading is making meaning. Even if they cannot read yet, they are engaging in early reading behaviors and see themselves as readers. This secure feeling will make it easier for the teacher to take them to the next level as readers. Each child learns he or she is now a part of a literate community.

Shannon Blaney is one of many teachers who engages her students in designing their class library. Building their library together introduces her first-grade students to the classroom collection, the concept of book genre, the organization of their library, and the expectation of maintaining that organizational system.

By the end of the first week of school, Shannon is ready to lead her class into setting up their library. The open meeting space at the front of the room is strewn with picture books from Shannon's personal collection and more from the school library. Plastic baskets are stacked haphazardly behind the books. (See Figure 2.1.) The children gasp and exclaim in shock at the mess as they come back into the room after lunch. Shannon asks them to sit down and gestures that they need to come up with a plan to solve this problem. From her actions, the children can tell that she wants to put the books in the baskets but does not know how to set about the task. Shannon starts by pulling four books in front of her. She points to the covers and says, "Hmmm! Lions. Alligators. Squirrels. Bears. What do you think?"

"They're all animals!" shouts Donte.

"Oh, you're right!" says Shannon. "What should I do with them?"

"Put the animal books in the same basket," suggests Caleb.

Shannon picks up an index card and writes the word *Animals*. She spreads out three sheets of mixed stickers and asks José to find some animal pictures and stick them on the card, which he does. José speaks few words of English but is able to understand Shannon's gestures. Shannon tapes the card to the front of a basket.

Next Shannon asks Uriel, Dat, Samia, and Nikki to find some more animal books. Nikki and Samia do this quickly, as Dat and Uriel look on. Shannon points again to the animal stickers on the card and to the books the girls have selected. Uriel catches on next, followed quickly by Dat. (Even though they have the least English of the class, Shannon has orchestrated this moment to allow Dat and Uriel to really understand their task.) Shannon asks all the students to look for any animal books to add to the basket. She labels another, asking Dat to find animal stickers this time.

Shannon continues sorting books in this way over the next few days, until all the books are stored in baskets along the wall. Later she tackles sorting the animal books into fiction and nonfiction baskets. Children are excited to see that there are also baskets for books in their first languages. All students are involved in the design of their precious classroom library. Shannon has orchestrated a wonderful community-building activity!

Talk at Your Table!

The children work at tables, not desks. Desks tend to isolate children. We want the children to be shoulder to shoulder so they can hear and see what others are doing. Copying other children is the way children first learn the routines. For example, watching other children sort and line up apples on a graph is the way a beginning ELL learns to graph. ELLs need to be close to their friends for visual learning.

Working at tables with six children encourages more talk than if children are at desks. Teachers with desks in the room can push six desks together with the open sides inwards to form a table. We make crayons, markers, scissors, and glue easily accessible in caddies on the tables for the simple reason that it also increases the talk in the room. When they need other supplies, children bring them to the tables. If they do not know the word for something they need, they can go and get it. If they do know the word, they can practice that vocabulary. Children drawing during writing workshop will say to someone at their table, "I need a red crayon." Second language learners will quickly learn the names of colors without the teacher having to teach color words in isolation.

Sitting at tables helps children learn manners and sharing. They learn to say simple phrases in English as they hear, "Gimme glue please" and "Thank you." Children can be very creative in their language. Maria said, "I need a new deleter." Someone at the table handed her an eraser.

Groups use the tables all day for workstations when working on art projects, science projects, math games, social studies posters, or other small-group activity. The amount of time a child might be at his or her "place" is limited. A table is more communal property than a single child's space—more of a small-group table than "my seat." Children surrounded by talk in this relaxed atmosphere are internalizing language and will soon attempt spoken English at their table.

When we plan our class seating arrangement, we first assign an English speaking role model to each table. Next, we assign children who are just acquiring English to each of these tables. Then we fill up all the tables with a mixture of boys and girls, all speaking various levels of English. At each table, we try to have at least one fluent English speaker. If two children speak the same language and have little English, we will often put them at the same table until they feel comfortable.

As we have mentioned before, our objective is to have a table where children will feel comfortable and safe. If a child who speaks only Farsi comes into the class late in the year, we will place that child near a Farsi speaker if possible. We have seen a native English speaker become best friends with a child who has the least amount of English. Language does not get in the way of friendship.

This does not mean that advanced English speakers or native English speakers serve mainly as role models or that we neglect their needs. These students also meet in a small group to challenge their thinking and enrich their vocabulary and comprehension. For instance, a class may be involved in an author study of Tomie dePaola with his amazing array of books in many genres. The class will have whole-group discussions and lessons about the craft of writing from many of his books. The whole class may be learning from his books during science time. During a study like this, we may pull a small group of children who have advanced language skills or who are native English speakers. Together they can explore dePaola books on legends, such as *The Legend of the Indian Paint Brush.*

Social and Emotional Environment

The teacher creates a social and emotional environment that allows the class to grow together as an inclusive community. She creates opportunities for the students to practice the necessary skills to develop this sense of community.

Morning Meetings: Learning to Be Part of a Community

To set the tone of each day, we begin with a morning meeting in which we engage all students in purposeful conversation that allows them to practice language structures. We design our morning meetings so that everyone can take part from the beginning. We go around a circle and everyone greets the group with "Good Morning." As the year progresses, the bar is raised as more language creeps into the ritual. For example, "Good Morning" may change to adding the person's name on either side while learning to make eye contact. Alex starts with greeting those on both sides of him. "Good morning, José. Good morning, Rashad." Rashad will continue with, "Good morning, Alex. Good morning, Levi." Levi picks it up with, "Good morning, Rashad. Good morning, Gina." This greeting might change later to Salaam Alaikum or Buenas Dias. Those who are not ready to speak aloud nod or whisper.

Quick morning meeting activities that are inclusive, low-stress, and work well for ELLs are:

- Rolling a ball across the circle and saying your name; later saying the name of the person you will roll the ball to; later saying "Good morning" and then the person's name.
- Adding the phrase, "I have something to share" after "Good morning."
- Learning to say good morning in several languages.
- Signing your name or putting a magnet with your name on it to answer a pictorial question. The answers make a graph. Do you like cats or dogs? Are you a boy or a girl? Discussing the results together as part of morning meeting.
- Using a choral reading, chant, song, or poem that becomes the daily class ritual.
- Finding native countries for all students on a map and marking each with a dot and the student's name.
- Using icons as well as words that illustrate the schedule of the day so that children will know where they are going and when. (See Figure 2.2.)
- Using a child's name in the morning message or asking a child to come up and write a letter or word he or she knows as the class writes the message together.

Figure 2.2 Adding a graphic to the schedule of the day allows all students to know what the afternoon holds for them.

For more activities we suggest reading *The Morning Meeting Book* by Roxanne Kriete.

In Kevan Miller's first-grade classroom, her children learn more about each other's families during a morning meeting. Kevan and the children are sitting in a circle. One at a time, the children turn to each other, shake hands, and choose a greeting to pass around. There is a mixture of Spanish and English. The greetings come full circle back to Kevan. She gently clarifies what she heard. "I heard 'good morning,' 'good afternoon,' 'ola,' 'hello,' and 'buenas tarde.' 'Good afternoon' is really nice and friendly, but morning is when you come to school. Now we should say, 'good morning.' After lunch we can say 'buenas tarde,' or 'good afternoon.'"

"You have been talking about your families." Kevan spreads out post-cards of art prints in the center of the circle and says, "I want you to pick a card that shows what's important about your family." Ronal immediately responds, "I don' know nothing 'bout my family." So Kevan says, "Think of something you like about your family." This time Ronal responds, "Oh yes, I know."

The children each pick a card. Choosing is hard so a few are holding a handful of cards. Someone takes one from another's hand so Kevan has to reinforce social skills. She reminds the children, "Take a card from the floor and not from your friend's hand." Meanwhile Ronal is trying to lie on as many cards as he can. Zihnab is counting cards.

Kevan says, "Time's up, so you have to sit back in the circle. Mirella, you have to choose one, you can't take them both." Kevan removes the extra cards and asks the children, "Do you remember how you did eye-to-eye and knee-to-knee?" She asks Karol and Christine, who are sitting next to each other, to model this for the class. They quickly face each other and cross their legs, letting their knees lightly touch. They look each other in the eye and smile. They do a great job, and the rest of the children spontaneously break into applause. Kevan then asks these two to turn from each other and face the child next to them in the circle ready to share. Now it is clear how the children will need to pair up, so she asks everyone to share why they chose their card.

Dr. Marie Clay writes in *By Different Paths*, "It is not a matter of first learning how to make communication work. Rather one has to get conversation underway in order to extend one's command of the language. It is the only way learning can take place." All Kevan's children seem willing to talk about their choices. Karol is holding Christine's hand as they talk. Karol is a native Spanish speaker. Christine is a Vietnamese newcomer who has learned a few words of English. Gavin is holding a picture of a ladder. He says, "My brother climbed up the ladder to get a Frisbee on the roof." His partner, Kennedy, is holding a picture that resembles butterfly wings, and shares, "My sister catched this butterfly on my arm. I got a flower and the butterfly came." After a few minutes, Kevan warns them that it is time to finish their conversations. She says, "I want you to get back to your spot by the count of three." The children squiggle back to the circle. Kevan says, "You were reminded of a lot of stories about your families, weren't you? Now I'm going to tell you what the morning will look like." She points to the words and pictures on the schedule. Karol quietly translates into Spanish for Jessica, a newcomer.

Kevan has provided visual models to communicate expectations. She has created a situation that provides a prompt around which children can build their conversation. Every child is able to participate in a conversation in a nonthreatening environment. And it is an economic use of time for a busy teacher. Starting the day this way lets everyone know they are a welcome and vital part of the learning community.

The Children Develop Rules to Live By

Shannon Blaney, who spent time with her students creating their library, had wanted everyone to have input into developing a set of class rules as she began to build her classroom community early in September. Shannon speaks Spanish, so she knew she could make the necessary concepts comprehensible to Uriel, a Spanish newcomer who had not yet acquired any English. However, Dat was a different story. He had recently arrived from Vietnam and like Uriel spoke no English. There were no other Vietnamese students in the class. Somehow, Shannon wanted to make the lesson visual and more concrete for both of these students, and for several others who were at the preproductive stage of acquiring English.

Shannon started with the question, "What do you want our classroom to be like?" and set out to draw from the children a picture of what they wanted.

She began by reading *David Goes to School* by David Shannon and asked, "Do you want it to look like this?" indicating the picture of David screaming. The children began to talk, and Shannon asked questions. She pointed to the pictures in the text to help some children understand. She expected a response from everyone but accepted a simple yes or no, a shake or nod of the head from Dat, Uriel, and José. (See Figure 2.3.)

Then she asked the students to draw on an index card a picture of what they wanted their classroom to be like. José was able to understand and draw the difference between "quiet" and "screaming." As she talked with Uriel, Shannon encouraged nods and whispers as input to the discussion. While the children continued with independent work, Shannon wrote on the cards and each student dictated what expectation was illustrated. When it was time to talk to Caleb about his picture, he was engrossed in drawing another picture to go with a story he was writing. Shannon asked Dat to go get Caleb. She handed him the index card, pointed to Caleb's name, and then pointed to a spot next to her. Dat went over to Samia and held out the card with a questioning look on his face, suggesting he wanted to know if she was Caleb. Samia pointed to Caleb. Dat went over to Caleb and tapped him on the shoulder. He handed him the card and then pointed to Shannon.

23

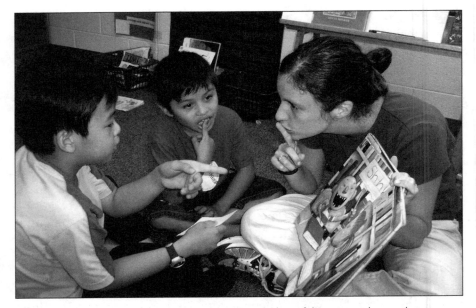

Figure 2.3 Shannon gives Dat and Uriel an extra reading of the story to deepen their understanding.

Although it had involved a little extra effort on her part, Shannon had been able to give Dat a task he could both understand and complete. The next time she asked him to get another student he would have this experience to build on, and the whole process would go more quickly. With the cards now prepared, the lesson would continue the next day.

The children and Shannon convened in a circle on the rug the next morning. Shannon placed the chart on the floor in the middle of the circle and spread out the children's index cards. Mishaal had been absent the previous day, so Shannon began the follow-up lesson by asking the children to update her. She gave everyone an opportunity to contribute. Next she asked the children to place their illustrated cards into at least one of three categories: take care of self, take care of each other, and take care of the school.

In order to do this, Shannon wrote at the top of a large piece of chart paper, "Our Class Promise." She quickly divided it into the three categories with a heading for each, explaining as she went along. It was quite straightforward to the English speakers, but she needed something visual to make it clear to the other students. Shannon picked up Chris's card on which she had written, "The children are sharing." Shannon said, "If I'm sharing with Chris, is it taking care of myself" (she hugs herself), "or is it taking care of each other?" (She hugs Chris.) They chose to put Chris's card under "take care of each other."

Shannon was mindful of how long she could expect first graders to sit still in those first days of school, so she sent the students off for their inde-

Figure 2.4 Shannon ensures that Dat and Uriel understand the rules by adding graphics to the newly written Class Promise.

pendent reading time. During this time, she worked with Dat, Uriel, and José, and with lots of pointing and miming was able to get them to add graphics to illustrate the words in each section: "self" (one stick figure), "each other" (two stick figures), and "school" (a building). (See Figure 2.4.) Later the children came to a consensus in sorting the other pictures, glued them in place, and then they all signed their names to their Class Promise. The chart hangs on the wall to refer to whenever anyone needs a reminder about expectations. In addition, teachers often make other charts with digital photos of children modeling expected behaviors.

Besides morning meetings, many teachers have class meetings to help solve class concerns such as noise level during writing workshop or the best number of children at the overhead center. These meetings start with children giving compliments and thanks to classmates, such as, "Thank you Huy, for helping me clean up the paint spill." After compliments, the teacher or a child brings a social concern to the group. The group works together to solve the problem. Having set the rules together at the beginning of the year, the class has a place to start in deciding the solutions. Jane Nelson's book *Positive Discipline in the Classroom* is very helpful in establishing class meetings.

In Emelie's classrooms, the class meetings start with a song. "I am special. I am special. If you look, you will see. Someone very special. Someone very special. That is me. That is me." Time for compliments and problem-solving follows the song. Her class puts closure on the meeting by standing and holding hands while singing, "The more we meet together, together, together, the more we meet together the happier we will be. 'Cause your friends are my friends, and my friends are your friends. The more we meet together the happier we'll be." We change the word *meet to read, sing, clean,* or *share* as needed.

A child at the preproduction or early production stage can participate in class meetings by bringing up a problem. One day after a lovely round of compliments, Giang uttered his first words. Pointing to Lucia he said, "He cut! He cut!" Even though he was pointing to a girl, we all knew what problem he was bringing to the group. Every child feels like part of the class when they discuss how to solve problems like this or when they raise their hand to vote on whether two or three people should play at the overhead center.

Nonverbal Ways to Help Children Feel Safe, Secure, and Welcome

When children come to our school, we have to know that they may never have seen a water fountain, ridden on a school bus, walked down a cafeteria line, eaten a pizza or hot dog, seen a fire alarm box, heard a fire alarm, or encountered a jack o'lantern. During all these new experiences, we have to be there gently for children in case they need us. This awareness and meeting of unspoken needs is the way a strong classroom community wraps its arms around newcomers.

Making sure children that have just arrived in our country are not the first in line at the water fountain on the first day and making sure they find something that is appealing to eat in the cafeteria is part of helping children learn to trust us and know that they are safe. During the first fire drill, we stand close to the newest children and are ready to comfort them. We warn them with hand signs what is coming. As we hold their hands, touch their shoulders, or stand next to them in line, the children know we will protect them.

Children often come in late in the year. We greet new students with their names already written at a table, their own coat hooks, book boxes, and journals. We sit them next to a child who speaks their language if possible. The class practices pronouncing new students' names correctly. Two students give a tour of the room. The rest of the day children squabble over who will get to take them through the lunch line, eat with them at lunch, be their friend at recess, introduce them to the music teacher, or buddy read with them. Having a language buddy or another student buddy can help children get through their first days.

A new student is like a breath of fresh air coming into the class. During the first day the teacher will make informal assessments as the child interacts with children, uses books, and participates in workshops. We will observe what he or she knows about books, reading, writing, math, and oral language. This helps us know where to start when planning for the child's instruction on the next day.

Some children experience a very rough beginning as they join our school community, and we have to work extra hard for them to feel safe and secure. Antony arrived at Tess's door one morning, midway through first grade. He was terrified, and his fearful crying made it difficult to continue teaching that morning. Thankfully, the other children were deeply concerned and patiently tried to help in any way they could. Antony survived lunch because Tess stayed at his side throughout the lunch period. A large cafeteria like ours has to move children quickly through the lines and out into a large seating area in order to operate efficiently, so it can be an overwhelming experience for young children, especially children new to our school culture.

Later that afternoon when Tess took the class to the gym for their PE lesson, Antony broke down again and clung to her as she tried to leave. Tess took him back to the classroom with her. They were both exhausted. She would need to come up with a plan to help both of them.

Tess remembered another student who had arrived under similar circumstances several years before. Julio was now in fifth grade. After school, Tess caught Julio and asked him if he would be willing to help her with Antony since he had been through a similar experience. Naturally, he said he would. Tess went to ask Julio's teacher if she could borrow Julio for some brief blocks of time over the next two or three days. She also checked with the PE and music teachers to make sure that they would not object to Julio accompanying the class to their lessons.

Julio waited with Tess the next morning to greet Antony, and he sat next to him in the circle as the class held their morning meeting. He rejoined them at lunchtime, and Antony was willing to sit next to him in the cafeteria. Once Tess knew Antony was calm, she was able to leave. Julio held Antony's hand as they went to the gym later that afternoon and stayed with him for PE. Because Julio was able to help Tess foster a sense of trust in Antony, the school experience became a little less frightening for him, and he gradually settled into the routine.

Emelie remembers when Huy arrived from Vietnam. At school, he was screaming and crying, kicking his feet on the floor, running away at recess, and pulling out his hair. She solved the problem by inviting his mother to come into the class and stay. For two weeks, Huy and his mother squatted together on the floor and learned about school in America. Later on during a home visit, Emelie discovered that his mother had learned to speak English by practicing the songs and poems on the charts Emelie had sent home.

They were hanging on the wall in the living room. Huy, now in high school, gives back to Bailey's through a service club called Raider Readers. Raider Readers is a club at our neighboring high school for ELLs, sponsored by their ELL teachers. The high school students choose and practice reading picture books for Bailey's kindergarteners. The students walk to Bailey's once a month to read and discuss the books with two or three children. This club benefits both high school and elementary students.

Negotiating Meaning Is Vital

From the moment English language learners enter our class we talk to them as if they could talk back to us. We include them in every class conversation. We use extended wait time and smile encouragingly. If they do not respond orally, we encourage them to point or use their bodies. Pointing, we say, "Show me." If they do nothing, we still smile and move on. We do not give up or ignore them.

ELLs are active participants in all parts of the day. We work at finding ways in which new students can participate that do not require oral language. They can collect dry-erase boards and markers, turn off the lights, or turn the pages in the Big Book. In a class performance, a child with preproduction English will have a speaking part with another child, chorally repeating a line like, "Wishy Washy, Wishy Washy." A coveted job is that of lighting technician.

When we as adult learners try to reach new understandings, grasp a complex idea, learn something new, we grapple with partially understood ideas and we use language to try to clarify meaning for ourselves. We do this automatically, using phrases such as "Let me get this straight . . . ," "What I hear you saying is . . . ," "Am I right in thinking . . . ?" As a conversation evolves, we are able to refine our understanding.

We do this with our students too. Our conversations continue all day long. Two of our closest colleagues, Kathleen Fay and Suzanne Whaley, express the importance of authentic conversations: "Authentic conversations with English language learners provide opportunities for teachers to clear up confusions, to teach strategies in meaningful contexts, to gauge comprehension, and to build a rapport with students" (2005, pp. 76–79). It takes time and talk to try to minimize the misunderstandings that naturally occur between people who are unable to speak the same language. Some of these misunderstandings are hilarious and some are more serious in nature and could cause distress or unhappiness.

Emelie once gave a parent a compliment about his child saying, "Pedro is so funny. He keeps us laughing all day." The parent interpreted the word *funny* as meaning his child was peculiar and thought that the class was laughing at his son. Emelie learned from this experience that it is sometimes helpful to have an interpreter available even if the parent is making good progress in English acquisition.

As children are learning English, there are many times in the day when we have to think hard and ask for clarification to develop meaning from their words. When Kelsi said, "Tall shoes," she was looking for high heels. When Jennifer skipped into the room asking, "Do you like my new piano pants?" she wanted to know if we liked her pink pajama pants. When Erik begged, "Can I play with the long necks?" he was waiting his turn to play with the dinosaurs. When José gleefully displayed his books and exclaimed, "Look what I got at the book bananas!" he was talking about our "Book Bonanza," a book giveaway at the end of the year. And there is always "D N," the end!

Teachers Model Respect for and Acceptance of Everyone

Children show respect for and acceptance of each other's English acquisition. This behavior comes from the teacher modeling it. Our individualized program during reading and writing workshop provides children with the opportunity to concentrate on their own literacy learning. Children understand that everyone's learning is different yet honorable. Each individual book box represents the hard work that each student is doing as a reader. Children know that their book boxes are special and are right for them. They know that we honor what is in their book boxes and we honor them as readers. They trust us to put the right books in the boxes for them.

During writing workshop, the children honor each other's attempts. They know that not all children have the same writing expertise but that all are learning what writers do. The class celebrates each writer's success because we have modeled celebrating each little step. Students know that they each have a different goal. They are confidant that we will celebrate their learning. Celebrating learning is a way we show respect for every child.

Our school has three rules: Respect yourself. Respect others. Respect property. Teachers throughout the building model what these rules mean so that all students understand how they apply in every situation.

Allowing Downtime or Alone Time for
English Language Learners

One way that we can respect our ELLs is to acknowledge their hard work of living daily in an environment that does not include their familiar home language. We acknowledge this by allowing the students to take some time out during the day. Listening to a new language is exhausting. Sometimes children need to go off alone for a while and listen to music or just relax. A listening center is essential. A second language learner can rest from the noise of the class by listening to tapes and CDs of songs, rhymes, and music. The listening center, used for movement and dance with the whole class earlier, can now be a respite area for a single child or a small group. The choices of books include books in various languages.

We have learned to accept that children sometimes seem to have just "turned us off." When children are first learning English, this often happens in the afternoon as they tire. We ignore the behavior. They are exhausted from trying to understand what is going on all day. As they learn more and more English, their endurance for attending will increase. We know that if we ignore it for a little while and let their brains rest, they will sit back up and tune us in again.

Sometimes we encourage students to take a break by painting, drawing, building with blocks, looking at books, or looking out the window. A quiet time can do wonders. A little rest curled up on a pillow might be all a child needs to be refreshed. In addition, listening to a tape in his or her language or painting with a friend who speaks the same language can revive the child's spirits. When we give a child permission to take a break, we are honoring his or her hard work. We are saying, "We know it is hard to live for seven-and-a-half hours with a new language all around you. You are doing a great job. Take a break and join us when you are ready."

Making the Classroom an Extension of Home and Family

A central part of making a room secure and safe for a child is making it feel like an extension of home. At our school, the children sit outside the classrooms in the morning, reading from baskets of magazines or books until it is time to come into the room. Many of the parents wait with their children. When some teachers invite the children into the room for the day, the parents also are encouraged to come in and work with the children for fifteen or twenty minutes.

During this "Parents as Teachers" time, parents have an opportunity to learn what an American school is like. The teacher and the parent form a bond during these morning sessions. Teachers give the parents a business card with school and class phone numbers as well as an email address.

Children place a picture of parents and children working together in the hallway as an invitation and visual for other parents, who come into the classroom and learn the names of the children and the plans for the day. The parents are anxious to learn English. Many received only a few years of education in their own country. They are eager to learn computer skills, math, social studies, science, or anything that we are studying.

When the parents and their children come into the classroom, there is something on the tables for them to do together: make patterns with pattern blocks, look and talk about the pictures in nonfiction books, use clay to form letters, count beans, or write numbers. Sometimes Emelie will direct these lessons from an overhead to teach the parents how to work with their children: "Let's make stick letters. Start at the top and go straight down making the letter *l*. Now let us make a *t*. Start at the top and go straight down. Now go left to right." The parents enjoy seeing the correct way to help their children at home.

When children are using clay to form letters or numbers, Emelie offers small bags of clay to the parents to take home. Emelie laughingly shows her muscles and uses other gestures. She is communicating that playing with clay helps develop small muscles in a child's hand. The parents happily walk out the door to go home after this early morning class time. They understand that if they let their children play with clay after school their children will hold the pencil and crayons better.

If we are rolling a number cube to practice counting, adding, or subtracting, we give the parents the number cube to take home to use with their children. Our parents want to help their children learn and are eager to do so. Inviting the whole family to be part of the learning community in the Parents as Teachers sessions benefits the parents by teaching them many ways to help their children at home. The sessions also give the children a loving start to their day. They have their parents sitting next to them playing a game, holding their hand helping them form a letter, encouraging them to count a little further, or reading them a book in their first language. What a lovely way to start the day for any young child! (See Figure 2.5.)

In first grade, Tess held an open house the first Friday of every month. The classroom was open to parents from a half hour before school started until a half hour after school finished. Parents were welcome to drop in whenever they could. Tess was available to talk before and after school. In December, and at the close of the year, the children planned a special breakfast for their parents.

An invaluable member of our staff is our Spanish-speaking parent liaison, Maria Demarest. Years ago, Maria stepped into her desperately needed position as a bridge between school and parents. Many other schools in our district have since created a similar position in their communities. Maria has expanded her role to become a one-woman provider of social services, trusted by everyone in and beyond the school.

Here is an e-mail sent by first-grade teacher Jodi Maher to the whole school, in which she expresses thanks and appreciation for Maria helping her expand her classroom community to the homes of her students:

Figure 2.5 Erick's father is overwhelmed with pride as he realizes that he and Erick can learn to read in English together.

I just wanted to share a wonderful experience I had this week. Ten of the seventeen students I have are Spanish speakers. Most of them come from homes where they speak only Spanish. All year I have been unable to call these parents and share something wonderful that their child did or even have a conversation in the hallway because I do not speak Spanish very well. I was telling Maria Demarest about this a few weeks ago and asked if I could invite these parents to come to the school for an informal gathering where we could exchange questions and stories about the children with her help. Maria took it from there. I gave her my list of ten students with phone numbers. She called each family and must have been very persuasive, because seven of them said they would come. The other three came in the morning as they dropped off their children to explain personally to me why they wouldn't be able to come. They came on Tuesday afternoon from 2:30 until dismissal and it was great. I was able to explain things (with Maria translating) and to get a better picture of what these students are like at home. I was very appreciative of the parents taking their time to come. They thanked me so many times for meeting with them, but I couldn't help feeling like the thankful one!

I am especially thankful that we have Maria here. She is a true liaison between our school and the families we serve here. She also has had so much experience here that she knew how much explanation was necessary—and even DEMONSTRATED how to read at home with a child! She was really wonderful. I would encourage everyone who is feeling frustrated about not being able to communicate with even ONE family, to let Maria know. She can help!

Tess replied:

And by coincidence, I was asking Maria to call one of these parents about one of my Reading Recovery students. I was able to join in the conversation. Maria took on so many roles as we have seen her do so often. She is a trusted friend who talks about parenting, instruction, supporting students at home, parental responsibilities in relation to sleep, homework, communicating with teachers, and so much more . . . with a large dose of joy and laughter thrown in.

Building a Community of Learners Takes Time

The first days and weeks are hard for both students and teachers. It takes the first few weeks of school for the class to learn all the routines and to feel comfortable in the room. The books we have read have been about friendship and solving problems together. The writing workshop lessons have been procedural. The math and science workshop lessons have concentrated on taking care of supplies, working in small groups, and reporting out.

Routines such as sitting eye-to-eye and knee-to-knee, sharing one marker with four children, and using dry-erase boards for work during lessons take practice and patience when the students are learning mostly by modeling. However, when children understand the routine of getting their book boxes out, sitting and reading independently somewhere in the room, and then moving calmly into buddy reading, the teacher can rejoice. The foundation of classroom community has been laid. The teacher who patiently and with a sense of humor has spent time nurturing her students as they build community can now move forward. She can begin to focus on small-group instruction, knowing that the children understand how to operate within their classroom community. The process of building community, however, continues every day throughout the year.

WORKSHOP:
THE ARCHITECTURE THAT SUPPORTS ENGLISH LANGUAGE LEARNERS

A second rationale behind integrating language and content teaching is that language is learned most effectively for communication in meaningful, purposeful social and academic contexts.

Patricia A. Richard-Amato and Marguerite Ann Snow,
The Multicultural Classroom

We talk and read and write across our days. The content of our lessons provides the hooks on which to hang all this talking, reading, and writing. We have learned that the workshop format provides the ideal vehicle in which we can all travel together, no matter what our needs. We can challenge our most advanced thinkers while including the newest arrival from another country in our lessons. In *Best Practice*, Zemelman, Daniels, and Hyde note that "teachers are beginning to extend the workshop model outward from reading and writing, where many have already found success, into other parts of the curriculum—establishing math workshops, science workshops, history workshops. They do this because whatever the content, deep immersion is the key to mastery: teachers want kids to *do* history, *do* science, *do* math."

We are strong proponents of this workshop model for several reasons. It fosters the individualized instruction that we implement in order to meet a wide range of academic and linguistic needs. It enables us to expose our ELLs to content through interactive experiences, with guided practice, during whole-group lessons. They then have opportunities to apply their learning in small-group settings. For a second language learner who is not ready to speak out in a whole group, the small group provides a less risky setting in which to try out new language.

Workshops in all areas of the curriculum follow the same pattern:

- Whole group, with literature as an introduction, transition, or review
- Mini-lesson
- Small-group or independent work
- Whole-group reflection, closure

Whole-Group Time and Mini-Lessons

We begin with our whole group gathered on the floor in front of us. A piece of literature provides our starting point. There will be "wonderings" and discussion as the story unfolds. A mini-lesson will follow. We have planned an explicit teaching point based on student need and curriculum requirements. The students will be actively participating at this time, building understanding through some kind of shared experience such as:

- Watching and helping with a demonstration;
- Using manipulatives to work through a problem;
- Acting out an event;
- Contributing to a shared writing experience;
- Engaging in a shared reading experience.

It is during this mini-lesson that we try to find ways to make our explanations more concrete and visual for our ELLs. Throughout this book we have included examples of how integration of the arts is beneficial to ELLs as a way of teaching language. The arts are a safe vehicle in which all students can learn. Visual and performing arts naturally differentiate, meet almost all learning styles, create a community of learners and risk-takers, stimulate higher-level thinking skills, create another opportunity for students to create and communicate meaning, and so on. We also create opportunities to model language structures so that they can listen and begin to internalize, or rehearse them if they are ready.

Leonel had rehearsed his first public statement well. As usual, his mother, Maria, had been spending the first half hour of her morning with Emelie's class. She was determined that Leonel would share his news at circle time just as the other students did. When she arrived at school on this spring morning, she indicated that she and Leonel had practiced what he would share all the way to school. Maria, with Leonel's little brother Pedro in tow, even sat next to Leonel in the circle, ready to prompt if necessary. When it came to his turn, Leonel needed to repeat the class ritual that led into each child's sharing. The routine of asking to share and being invited to do so had happened over and over since school began. Ythrip turned to Leonel, who as usual was waving his hand in the air. "Good morning, Leonel." "G'morning, Ythrip. I have something to share." A sudden stillness fell. Maria and the class held their collective breath. Ythrip asked, "Do you want to share it?" "Yes please. My tooth came out." The class broke into applause, Maria heaved a sigh of relief, and Leonel beamed. It took time, patience, practice, and the support of a caring community to bring Leonel to this point.

Small-Group or Independent Work

Now we wish to give the students time to follow up with opportunities to try out what they have just learned, or review other work from previous mini-lessons. We might assign tasks, or the work might involve student choice. But this is a time of active engagement. We are going to hear a high level of conversation during this part of the lesson. We ourselves will be teaching a small group or conferring with a child as others listen in. Meanwhile the children are explaining their pictures to friends, asking for help, sharing information, correcting each other, expressing and revising ideas, making plans, or describing their thinking. They are coming to understanding through talk.

Small-group or independent work might involve such activities as:

- Testing a scientific hypothesis;
- Playing math games to reinforce a skill;
- Solving math problems with manipulatives;
- Working on a mural to show continents and oceans;
- Role playing at an experience center: using money at the store, acting out flower pollination, reenacting a story;
- Reading independently or with a buddy;
- Writing: stories, math journals, science logs;
- Practicing reading and writing work at literacy centers.

Reflection and Closure

After this period of collaboration, we call the children back to the meeting place. It is time to share and reflect on our learning. The children share their work or their thinking, and the other students ask questions or give comments or suggestions. A second language learner might bring a new understanding to the group but be unable to express it orally. We can frame this understanding in language for him or her.

One day during Emelie's writing workshop, Erick was drawing and writing about a car. His usual car picture had a new dimension, but Emelie could not understand what he had drawn or wanted to write. He had carefully drawn blue all around his car and written the pattern sentence, "I like the car."

"Erick, I see you drew about a car today." Erick smiled and mumbled something unintelligible. Pointing to the blue, Emelie asked, "What is this blue?" Erick shrugged his shoulders. "Is it the road? The street?" Erick shook his head. Pointing to the sky, Emelie continued, "Is the car up in the sky? Did the car go up in the sky?" Erick shook his head again, and then he stood up and held his breath, puffing out his cheeks. He began to windmill his arms around as if he was swimming. Now Emelie understood him. "Oh, water," she exclaimed. "Your car crashed in the water." Erick nodded delightedly as he repeated, "Water. Water. Car crash!"

Literacy Centers

Since literacy centers play such a large role in our day, we want to go into these in a little more detail. In kindergarten, literacy centers are open during free-choice learning-center time. And in both kindergarten and first grade, you will see the students working together on a range of open-ended literacy activities during workshop time. These kinds of reading and writing activities provide invaluable opportunities for the ELLs to engage in literacy work at their own level. It also provides time for teachers to observe and assess. Therefore, we need to make sure that the students are clear about which activities they can choose. Each center provides a social setting for language to occur. Children are practicing and learning both social and academic language as they converse with a friend: "Let's put this song up." "I found the letter *b*." Even those at the preproduction stage may be silent but are hearing the language and learning to comprehend or are engaged in learning through their first language.

Our centers include, but are not limited to:

- *Magnetic Letters*. Activities, based on assessment of student need, might include: sorting matching letters, matching upper-case and lower-case pairs, sorting for letter features (stick letters, circle letters, letters with tails, and so on), making students' names, making high-frequency words, changing onsets or rimes (for example, *c–at b–at f–at*, or *ca–t ca–n ca–r*).

- *Songs on the Overhead*. Our overhead sits on the floor so a small group of students can put transparencies of favorite songs up. We make sure to use a large clear font when we type these. Sometimes one student will act as teacher and point with a chopstick to the words on the overhead or up on the screen, as they all sing along.

- *Poem Charts*. We add new poems to our collection weekly. We tape coat hangers to the back of chart paper and hang them on a chart stand. Children are free to put them on the floor or read them as they hang.

- *Pocket Chart Activities*. The children can sort class names alphabetically, or into categories identified by pictures, such as boys and girls; or skirts, shorts, and long pants; or others generated by the students. They can also add missing words to a rhyme on sentence strips in the pockets, while referring to a copy of the rhyme posted next to the pocket chart if necessary. We use these same pocket charts at other times of the day. Second language learners can be successful as they sort concepts in science, math, or social studies: animal pictures to be sorted by fur, feather, and fins in science; fractions during math; sorting pictures of long ago and today or sequencing pictures of change over time in social studies. When children are working with a peer at these pocket-chart activities, they are practicing and learning language.

- *Dry-Erase Boards*. We provide children with individual sized dry-erase boards so they can all be actively engaged in the lesson. They use them to sign in, practice names, practice letters, write known words, practice new words, write their own morning message. (We use dry-erase boards at other times of the day: when solving math problems, predicting science experiments, and so on).

39

- *Listening Center.* Here we have books on tape in English and Spanish, songs, nursery rhymes, and restful music. The purpose of this center can be to reinforce language development or to provide a time to rest from the new language.

Managing Centers

It is important to consider how to manage activity choices so that the centers run smoothly and the children are productively engaged in an activity that meets their needs. We begin to familiarize the children with our centers early in the year, introducing one at a time. We introduce each one to the whole group, modeling the range of options at that center. We practice the activity as a whole class if possible. If this is not practical, we might introduce it to one small group at a time until everyone has had a chance to work at the activity. We often practice at centers in a structured group rotation to begin with. However, once the children are familiar with the procedures and expectations for each center, it becomes just one more reading or writing choice that is available in the room.

Literature as an Underpinning to Our Workshops

Oral language is the foundation of our workshops, the mortar that holds the components of both writing and reading across the curriculum together. Talk is essential to the learning that goes on in our classrooms, and you will hear the constant buzz of chatter there. We set out to foster opportunities for children to engage in conversation. (See Figure 3.1.)

They rehearse familiar language patterns in the morning circle, "Good morning. My name is . . ."; or at writing share time, "Do you have a question or comment?"; or during the read-alouds, "Who's that trip-trapping over my bridge?" They experiment with unfamiliar structures and new vocabulary. Storytelling is woven in throughout the day: personal stories, familiar stories, and stories snatched from the air of our imaginations.

We nurture this storytelling by relating the happenings in our own lives as well as the ones in the stories we read. In a 2005 *Language Arts* article on storytelling, Martha Horn says, "Through storytelling, we create a listening space, a place for children to tell their stories and to listen to each other; a place to find their words and craft their worlds into story" (83, 1: 33–41).

In the series that Lucy Calkins wrote with colleagues entitled *Units of Study for Primary Writing,* she, too, addresses the importance of story: "In order for children to write stories, they need to be immersed in a storytelling culture. Too many children don't have opportunities at home to regale their

Figure 3.1 Jodie Maher has planned the art activity to create opportunities for James, Ramza, and Shakera to talk as they share supplies and make decisions.

parents with little narratives from their day, nor do they hear parents retelling the funny, sad, or important moments of their lives. It is crucial, then, that schools provide opportunities for children to tell stories to each other, and to hear stories told by authors and teachers and peers."

Literature abounds across the curriculum and throughout the day. For our ELLs it provides a means of developing understanding. The pictures provide support. The stories help to build background knowledge. Story sequence and language are absorbed. So choosing the right books is extremely important.

Choosing Books That Interest Everyone

Recently Tess and Suzanne Whaley, our reading teacher, were chatting about books that children really enjoy. Tess shared a story about a book she'd read one year to a first-grade class called *Saving Sweetness* by Diane Stanley. It was the first time she had come across this story, and she really enjoyed reading it. She was fascinated by the way in which real photographs had been superimposed onto the illustrations and was tickled by the way the sheriff in the story kept thinking he was saving Sweetness when, all the time, Sweetness was saving him. Tess also enjoyed watching the children's faces as they came to realize this. After she had read the story, Nathaly had asked if she could look at the book. From that moment on, she did not put

41

the book down for a moment except when she went home, and then she picked it up as soon as she came into the classroom in the morning. She tucked that book under her arm and took it literally everywhere she went for three days.

Tess laughed as she told Suzanne about Nathaly, and Suzanne replied, "Well, you know why she did that, don't you?" Tess must have looked puzzled because Suzanne continued, "Obviously she could tell how much you enjoyed reading the story, and that's what made it so important to her." It has remained an important book for Nathaly as she has borrowed it several times since then. She came back to borrow it from Tess again this year to read with her younger sister. Nathaly has just completed sixth grade!

We find that ELLs will sit and listen to good literature even if they cannot understand the story line because they enjoy the experience of being together with their classmates, the rhythm, the drama, the expressions on the reader's face, the changes in voice, and the illustrations. We choose books that *we* love to read so that we are engaged in the reading as well as books that have illustrations that will engage all the listeners. We watch to see which books the children are enjoying during book browsing time or which ones they reread during independent reading time and will read them later to the whole class.

We choose books of high interest: about animals or ones with songs or rhythms, beats and rhyme. We choose ones that are sad, funny, repetitious and ones we can act out in the room and on the playground. We try to find books from every culture or country represented by the children in our classes. For example, we use *The Lotus Seed* by Sherry Garland for Vietnam, *Crow Boy* by Taro Yashima for Japan, *A Day's Work* by Eve Bunting for Mexico, all the Carlos books by Jan Romero Stevens for our Spanish students, *The Color of Home* by Mary Hoffman for Somalia, *Iguana Beach* by Kristine Franklin for Guatemala. The children are especially excited when the books are in their first language. (See Figure 3.2.)

We read lots of nonfiction and teach the children how to read the pictures for information; then we give them lots of practice, first, listening to others infer from pictures and then, trying it themselves. We choose Big Books, poetry, and sing our favorite songs together over and over again. As we read all this material, we know that our ELL students will not understand all of it, but that over time, their understanding will grow.

We select books for every area of the room and make them accessible to the children all day. (See Figure 3.3.) Along with choosing books, we learn to be observers of what our class likes each year. We are then able to select books based on student interests and needs. We also become observers of children as they interact with books on their own. When the students come into the classroom in the morning, which books or magazines do they

Figure 3.2 Aya scans the books in the school library looking for the ones written in Arabic. Parents appreciate that children can check out books in their first language.

reread? Which books are they chatting about during book browsing time? Which Big Books are falling apart because the children reread them so often? What are the favorite songs that they sing under their breath as they walk down the hall? Which types of nonfiction books are holding their attention?

As we listen to children chatter about books and characters, as we see them slip favorite books into their book boxes, hide a book to read later, or

Figure 3.3 Children search for the high-frequency word *went* as they retell a story with puppets.

race to get a book before anyone else can get it, we know that these are the books of high interest to our children. We then select these books to build further understanding and develop oral language for our ELLs through rereadings, drama, mini-lessons, and references during the day. All these experiences provide opportunities to rehearse the language they hear in books and to make connections to the stories. We also read other books in that genre or by the same author.

It is important for children to know that we choose books for a reason. Teacher attitude plays a big part in children being interested in the chosen books. When we present a book to the students, we let them know why we chose it. We let them know that we know what books they like and that we are going to help them make meaning of the book. "I picked out this book to read because I know that Jovanka wants to know more about why bubbles float." or "I'm going to reread *Heckedy Peg* by Audrey Wood today because I've seen some of you playing Heckedy Peg at recess, and I thought you might want to listen again to how Audrey Wood said the scary parts. Maybe others will want to listen closely to the words and join in the fun at recess."

One morning after picking up the book *Inside Mouse, Outside Mouse* by Lindsay Barrett George in the library, Emelie said, "I was in the library this morning and I saw this book. I looked at the cover then sat right down and read it. I thought, 'my class is going to love this book.' Guess what? You are the first class in the whole school to hear it. You'll love it. Are you ready?"

Few young learners can refuse that offer!

Supporting ELLs in Comprehending Text

Jeffrey, now in third grade, recently asked Tess, "Do you still cry when you read that book about the boy and the old man?" After some thought, they concluded the book was *Silver Packages* by Cynthia Rylant. Tess had read it to her class when Jeffrey was in first grade as an emergent English speaker. For several days, he begged her to read it to the third-grade writing group she was working with. Tess agreed, although she warned them this book never failed to move her. She managed to read the story without crying, but Jaime, who did not know the story, said, "You're making *me* cry," as he wiped his eyes. Jaime and Jeffrey will probably remember this story for a long time. In fact, a few days after this, Jeffrey asked another former classmate, Dallana, if she remembered the story that made Mrs. Pardini cry in first grade. "Oh yes, the one about the golden boxes [which was how she remembered the silver packages]," she said, matter-of-factly. Some of our favorite stories stay with us forever.

Silver Packages tells of a man involved in a car accident in Appalachia who is cared for by local residents. In order to repay them, he travels to the mountains by train each year bringing gifts for the children. One boy, Frankie, dreams for years of getting a doctor's bag, but he never does. He leaves the mountains but later, as an adult, returns to his native home and watches the children run after the Christmas train. A little girl falls and hurts herself. Frankie runs over, puts down his doctor's bag, and tells her he will take care of her.

When Tess read this story in first grade she knew that Jeffrey and Dallana had understood the story. They had participated in the class discussion after hearing it. The talk had been rich and reflective. Some of the English speakers had made many connections to their own lives and to other stories they had read. This conversation had provided a scaffold for the ELLs to construct their own meaning. One boy had told of his uncle getting hurt in a car accident, and this helped Jeffrey understand what had happened to the character in *Silver Packages*.

As the children joined in the discussion, Tess was able to assess to what degree they understood the story. Even Silvana, who spoke only Spanish at the time, was completely engaged in a way that was quite appropriate for a student in the "silent" or preproductive stage of language aquisition. She sat attentively throughout the story and discussion. Her eyes never left the pictures. During the discussion, she watched the speakers carefully.

At the time, Tess did not realize just what an impact this story had had on Jeffrey and Dallana. It was not only that they remembered their teacher being moved to tears as she read, but also that as a community the class had shared an emotional connection to that book that made it so memorable.

Fostering Understanding Through Careful Book Choice

We realize both the choice of the book and the way in which we approach it before, during, and after the reading can help make the meaning more accessible to the ELLs. Choosing and presenting books takes time and thoughtful planning.

It is so important to choose books that we care about and that we think will engage the students. The books we choose for our workshop must illustrate the teaching point of the mini-lesson, based on our assessment of student need. (We will talk more about mini-lessons and student assessment later.)

Next, we have to make sure that the book will capture the interest of our ELLs as well as the other students. Much of the meaning will come from the pictures. It will need striking illustrations. They might be realistically painted, colorful, amusing, beautiful photographs, or of high interest to the class.

The pictures must clearly support the text to help tell the story. We will often need to point to these pictures while reading in order to clarify something in the story, or indicate an unfamiliar vocabulary word without interrupting the flow of the story.

Take a moment to look at how a story unfolds in a wordless book. In the book *Home* by Jeannie Baker how will children know what is happening? Looking at the pictures by themselves without the words allows us to see how much the ELLs will get out of the story.

Interacting During Read-Alouds to Foster Understanding

As skillful readers, we anticipate both content and language structure as we read. The ability to predict events and language is going to make the task of reading easier for our youngest readers. Therefore, we want to model the importance of predicting the story as we read aloud, using language appropriate for that genre of text.

For example, in reading *Stellaluna* by Janell Cannon, we might ask, "What do you think Mama Bird said when she came home and saw her baby birds hanging by their feet?" "What else could she say?" "And look here. Mama Bird wants Stellaluna to promise something. Can you guess what Stellaluna will have to do if she wants to stay in the nest?" Our students expect to be involved in an ongoing conversation as we think about the book together. Our challenge as teachers is to balance this anticipatory thinking without disrupting the flow of the story.

One of our reading teachers, Kathleen Fay, has been working in Michelle Gale's kindergarten room this year. To allow opportunities for all children to participate at discussion time, she has practiced the routine of sharing eye-to-eye and knee-to-knee. When Kathleen tells the children to turn to a partner and talk about something, they know exactly what to do without wasting a moment.

In January, Tess had heard Marie Clay speaking at a conference. In her discussion of transitions faced by children first entering school, Dr. Clay had emphasized that telling stories is as important as hearing stories in preparing children for learning to read and write. This had led to some discussion back at Bailey's, and Kathleen was interested in helping these kindergarteners, most of whom were second language learners, develop a working system of storytelling. On this occasion, Kathleen had come with the illustrations of a wordless book prepared on overhead transparencies. The book was *Fetch*, an Oxford Reading story by Robert Hunt and Alex Brychta. In this story Floppy and his family are watching a woman throw sticks into a pond for her dog to retrieve. Mom tries to get Floppy to chase a stick into the pond but he refuses. But when Bobbie's hat blows into the pond, Floppy immediately rushes in after it.

The overhead projector was on the floor. Kathleen sat next to it, and the kindergarteners sat clustered in front of her.

Kathleen first told the story to the children, pointing to the pictures as she went, to model how to tell a story. "One day, Floppy and his family went to the park. It was a windy day." Then she went back to the beginning of the story, in order to engage the children orally, asking them to contribute ideas and dialog.

Kathleen asked, "How do you know it is a windy day?"

"'Cuz those things are blowing," David said, pointing to the leaves and branches.

"How do you know Floppy is thinking?" asked Kathleen. "What do you think Floppy might be thinking?

Reuben's hand shot into the air. "He no want to be wet!" he said.

"That's right, Reuben. Floppy might think, 'I don't want to get wet.' Or 'I don't want to go in the water.' He looks like he's doing this," and she turned her head sharply to one side.

Kathleen and the children all pretended to be Floppy turning his head away from the pond. Next Kathleen asked, "What is Bobbie thinking right now? Turn to a partner and tell him or her what you think Bobbie is saying." With a minimum of fuss, each child turned to face a partner and chattered eagerly about Bobbie. After two minutes, Kathleen quieted the children and asked for one or two suggestions.

Maria said, "Why Floppy no go like that dog?" Kathleen affirmed, "Yes, those dogs are having fun, aren't they?"

José chipped in with, "Her think Floppy scary by water." "Hmm, you're right, José." Kathleen responded, "He might be scared of the water."

"Oh, look here. What could Mom say?" Kathleen continued. Erin thought that she might say, "Oh Bobbie, your hat is blowing away."

"What could Bobbie say here?" pointing to Bobbie's smiling face. "What do you think, Yonathan?"

"Good," offered Yonathan.

"I have another one. 'Hooray!'" added David.

Reuben said, "Bobbie say, 'Floppy, thanks for getting my hat.'"

"Let's all practice saying that," and the children chorused after Kathleen.

Again, Kathleen asked the children to turn and talk to a partner to infer what Floppy might be saying. Kathleen closed the lesson by telling the children she had numbered the illustrations in order and that she would leave them at the overhead center so that they could practice telling the story with their friends at center time.

Rereading Familiar Stories to Deepen Understanding

It is also important to remember how much young listeners enjoy hearing familiar stories over and over. Our ELLs will anticipate favorite pictures even if they do not fully understand the story at first. They might even understand the story from the pictures, constructing it in their own language. By hearing the story again, they can take what they already know and begin to focus on attending to the language rather than the meaning. Watching their classmates' reactions will bring them closer to understanding. Each time they see and listen to a story, they will understand a little more. It is important that ELLs have the opportunity to hear the way a story sounds when read aloud. Even if they are exhausted from trying to cope with life in a foreign language, it is important that they feel the language flow over them in the reassuring safety of their class community. Tess and her brother both remember falling asleep to the sound of their father's gentle voice reading *Robinson Crusoe* at bedtime. We think this lull of narrative must also be comforting to children learning a new language.

In order to help different levels of language learners understand more of the book prior to reading we might

- Briefly summarize the story before we begin reading;
- Preview a few of the pictures to highlight some points in the story;

- Set the scene and through discussion, activate the prior knowledge the students bring to the topic;
- Clarify any potentially difficult vocabulary ahead of time, using the illustrations, or pictures in another text or actual objects;
- Give students a focus to think about, particularly if it is the second or third time they have heard the story;
- In nonfiction text, go over the essential vocabulary before, during, and after reading the book by sketching, pointing to pictures, simplifying language, or acting it out.

Let us think for a moment about one of our favorite stories, *Hattie and the Fox* by Mem Fox. It is such a well-illustrated story, that by adjusting our tone of voice, the children can tell that we are anticipating the climax. During the reading, we use a dramatic storytelling voice, facial expressions, eye contact, and body movement to communicate the story and encourage participation. We can raise the ceiling when we all "Moo!" at the end of the story! This book is such fun to read with children who are just learning English—the pictures tell the story. The children love to join in with the animals' repetitive responses, and we can go to town as Hattie as she discovers what is hiding in the bushes. Each rereading, each retelling, and each reenactment of this story helps to deepen the children's understanding and build their oral language.

Tess might introduce Natalie Kinsey-Warnock and Helen Kinsey's story, *The Bear That Heard Crying*, in the following way:

- *Activating Prior Knowledge.* "This story tells about a little girl, Sarah, who gets lost. Has anyone here ever gotten lost? Where did you get lost? How did you feel? What did your Mom and Dad do when they couldn't find you? What happened when they did find you?" And, "Look at Sarah's family here and on this page. Do you think this story takes place today? What makes you think this happened a long time ago?"
- *Making Connections.* "Yes. It reminded me of the pictures in *Yonder* by Tony Johnston too.
- *Setting the Scene.* "I'm going to introduce you to some of the important characters in this story. Here is Sarah and her family. This is Mr. Heath who finds Sarah."
- *Raising Anticipation.* "And you will never guess who takes care of Sarah when she is lost! Listen to find out!"

One thing we like to do to add meaning to the story for our ELLs is to act all or part of it out with the class. We could arrange a full dramatic retelling of *The Bear That Heard Crying*, or we could say, "Matt, would you and Jorge show us how Mr. Heath told about his dream to Joseph Patch?" Alternatively, as we point to the relevant picture we could say, "All of you, show me Joseph's face when he finds out Sarah wasn't with her parents."

In their book *Whole Language for Second Language Learners*, Freeman and Freeman say, "Acting out situations that do not occur naturally in the classroom is another way teachers can provide context" (1992).

We know that not every child understands every book or poem that we read. Emelie has seven grandchildren. When it is the oldest grandchild's turn to select a book, she does not say, "No, I can't read you that one because it is too hard for the others to understand." She just reads it to her, and the others enjoy the pictures and the flow and beauty of the language. When it is the youngest grandchild's turn to pick a book, the oldest grandchild enjoys the familiarity of the text or warmth of sharing a book together.

The same is true when we read a variety of text in the classroom. The teacher's job is to present each book as a special gift to the class—books that the class can enjoy, learn from, reread, and understand in their own way. Books thoughtfully chosen will offer rich oral language experiences to all our students. Throughout the school year, the children build meaning from these books to help them make sense of the world around them and lead them to new understandings.

Helping ELLs Participate in Discussion

Several years ago, Emelie watched a television documentary about how young children learn to participate in discussions. During the program, the camera recorded several children of different ages sitting at their dining-room table at suppertime. The children were listening, speaking, and interrupting each other during a discussion with their parents. What caught Emelie's attention was the way the youngest child, who was not yet talking, sat turning his head back and forth to watch each speaker's face intently. Emelie often thinks of that child as she watches her ELLs in her classroom, and she feels more comfortable allowing them time to just watch, listen, and participate silently as they, too, intently watch the speakers' faces.

This happened this year with Leonel. He closely followed each class discussion with his eyes. He raised his hand at every opportunity, but, although his eyes twinkled and he smiled impishly, it was not until the spring that he was able to communicate when called upon. Emelie honored his need for time.

In order to include our ELLs in the book discussion, we must first read the text dramatically, using voice, facial expressions, and body language to help convey the meaning. The ELLs are going to pay close attention to this, as they know from experience this is one way to gain some meaning about the book. They will also attend to the expressions and body language of their peers.

In order to answer a question, our second language learners might copy an expression or movement they have seen during the reading of the text. They can retell through acting out an answer, either alone, in a small group, or as part of the whole class, depending on their confidence. They will often join the class in chanting a phrase from the story or a fact from a piece of nonfiction. In response to a question, they might repeat a rehearsed phrase, give a favorite character's name, or perhaps just offer a sound effect. We must also create ways to allow our ELLs to participate in all our classroom discussions, not just those centered on story, but perhaps classroom or playground expectations, solving a math problem, or predicting what might happen in a science experiment.

Emelie's class enjoyed the many books in Joy Cowley's *Mrs. Wishy-Washy* series this year. The characters became very familiar to all the students. Children learned to chant "Wishy Washy! Wishy Washy!" and "Oh, lovely mud!" They never seemed to tire of these phrases. In the spring, "lovely mud" showed up in conversations and in their written text. These favorite chants were appropriate ways of participating in a discussion.

The degree of support we need to offer becomes clearer as we get to know our students better. We need to be aware of what language and understandings the students control or almost control. Then we will know how much support to offer in order for the ELLs to participate successfully in a discussion. Before Leonel shared the information about his lost tooth earlier, he had needed to listen to those same phrases repeatedly, perhaps eventually rehearsing them silently in his head. He had rehearsed aloud with his mother over and over. Most simply, we can enable student participation in a discussion by asking questions ELLs can answer, bearing in mind their control of English. Therefore, the question could require a simple yes or no answer and be supported by teacher pantomime or pointing to an illustration. "Here is King Bidgood. Is he going to get out of the bath *this* time?" We can rephrase questions or offer prompts to guide students' thinking. "What happened when the middle-sized Billy Goat Gruff crossed the bridge?" can be rephrased, with more support, "Look here is the middle-sized Billy Goat Gruff," pointing to the picture. "Here is the troll. What is the troll going to do?"

We offer wait time that is appropriate for each student to respond to a question. Some need much more time than others do. Then we might gently prompt with phrases such as, "Remember when . . . ," "Think about . . . ," "Look at this picture and think about . . . ."

When a child meets us with silence, we will say, "Show me in the book what you mean." If the student clearly needs more help, we might say, "Turn to the friend next to you. I want you to sit eye-to-eye and knee-to-knee and talk about this part of the story." This pairing allows the ELL to get an idea from a partner or rehearse an answer. Then we would ask the question again.

Sometimes we use a "quick question" technique where all the children answer the same question. "Do you agree with José that Mean Jean, the Recess Queen will move away? Or do you predict, like Jesse, that Mean Jean will make friends?" (Mean Jean is from *The Recess Queen* by Alexis O'Neill.) Every child quickly answers in turn either "Move!" or "Make friends!" Some children will give an explanation with their answers, and others will just say the one- or two-word answer. Everyone takes part in the conversation during quick questions. If an ELL is still in the silent phase, the answer might be a nonverbal response: such as a nod, smile, blink, or shrug.

To provide even greater support we could pair the student with another student who speaks the same language. The children could then discuss and reply in either their own language or English. We are not trying to force the student to speak English. Instead, we are trying to provide enough support to allow the child to understand and participate successfully. Finally, we could offer a graceful way out of a stressful situation by saying, "Would you like to choose a friend to help you think about this?" One of our colleagues, Pat Irwin, taught us to allow children to respond to a question by saying, "Still thinking," if they were not ready to answer.

ELLs need many opportunities for listening to others talk about books all day. Maybe a child will not feel confident talking in a large group. However, they will speak out with one adult or in a group of two or three children. This year Tess worked with small groups of third-grade ELLs. These children had been learning English since kindergarten. In the writing lab with Tess, they enjoyed lively discussions about the daily read-aloud. If Mrs. Frey, our principal, stopped by with some visitors, the children would cheerfully include them in their discussion of the book. However, back in the classroom some of them participated as little as possible in a large-group discussion. This kind of evidence shows that creating a safe environment is important to give our ELLs the experience of contributing when they want to.

The English language learner's contribution to a discussion will come. The first comment could occur during the discussion of a math book or a science book or with a resource teacher. As teachers, we need to be patient observers and maintain contact with all the adults who work with each student. A quick question to the music teacher in the hallway might bring unexpected surprises. "Mario, quiet? Then you would have been amazed to see him today. He was singing out at the top of his voice during music." And yet this student talks so softly during your circle time that you can barely decipher what he is saying. For this student the joy of expressing rehearsed language musically when everyone is participating is a much safer experience than being asked to generate language alone and in front of an audience in the classroom.

While we are waiting for the verbal contributions during our book discussions, we watch for the nonverbal ones. We take mental note of smiles, nods, headshakes, shrugs, sighs, and glances. We do not know what ELLs comprehend as they listen to the English discussions around them, or what English words, phrases, or conversations they are rehearsing in their heads, but we consider them full participants in our conversations.

As teachers, we must have patience with each child and the varying progress of language acquisition. We know that the child's participation during book discussions will gradually change. The child whose eyes travel from speaker to speaker or whose body leans silently forward to get a little closer will change into a hand waving, bouncing-in-place, shouting-out-responses child.

Assessing What Students Know and Deciding What to Teach Next

If oral language is the foundation of our workshops, then the foundation of all our teaching across the day is assessment. In her book, *By Different Paths to Common Outcomes*, Dr. Marie Clay includes this condition that applies to good communication: "The speaker has to be sensitive to the listener. You have to adapt your message to take account of who the listener is, what the listener already knows, and what the listener needs to know. Then you have to monitor the listener's behavior to work out whether you are being understood and the message is getting across. You look for signs that your listener is understanding you" (1998). This is how we assess.

Without ongoing assessment, we would have no idea of what to teach next and to whom, and so we weave assessment throughout the day. How do we assess our students who speak little or no English? How can they show us what they know? What tools will be most useful to us? What tasks can we develop that will illustrate their capabilities? We need to consider these questions carefully.

Since we want our assessment to be authentic, we do not use work sheets or written assessments for this purpose. We rely heavily on anecdotal evidence of what a child knows, along with an assortment of measurement continuums developed by our school division; rubrics, benchmarks, and checklists developed within our school at the team level; and systems we have developed ourselves.

We look at writing samples, record letter names and sounds that the children know, record which high-frequency words they know or almost know. We take and analyze running records to see which reading strategies they control as readers and which they are neglecting so that we know what to teach them next. Since fluency is important because it not only makes the reading sound good but it helps the reader anticipate the meaning, language structure, and vocabulary of the text, we also note how the reading sounds while taking running records.

Much of our teaching in response to this record-taking will be done through a morning message, a piece of shared writing that can occur in any of the content areas. If you were to walk into any primary classroom in our building, you would see a morning message up on a large whiteboard or large sheet of newsprint. It is clearly printed using large letters and well-defined spaces between words. It includes some of the words most frequently used by young writers. Sometimes the teacher writes the message before the children arrive, and sometimes they compose and write it together. The morning message clearly links reading and writing for the children, and it never ceases to amaze us what a wonderful teaching vehicle it is. It can also serve as a review or as a springboard into new learning and is used across the curriculum.

By writing and reading the message, we are able to teach the mechanics of writing: letter identification, letter formation, capitals and punctuation, hearing sounds in words, and spelling. We can also teach the craft of writing: composing, using strong leads, good endings, interesting words, writer's voice, writing in the style of a well-known author, and so on. We can teach to a wide variety of needs during this time. A newcomer might be learning the letters of her name, while another student is working on some high-frequency words, while yet another might be learning to write dialog.

The children are eager to read and reread this message as it is of high importance to them. It is about them or it gives them information about their day. When we reread the message, we think aloud about the reading strategies we are using: Does it look right? Does it sound right? Does it make sense? Did we read it with expression, or did we sound like robots? Did we read it smoothly or did it sound choppy? (To learn more about teaching literacy with a morning message, we would recommend reading *Getting the Most Out of Morning Message and Other Shared Writing* by Carleen Payne and Mary Schulman.)

We believe that a child's learning should be woven together through the sharing of literature in a workshop format that optimizes oral language development. We agree with Peregoy and Boyle that "language development should be vocal and visible in classrooms where talk is valued as a learning tool" (1997). All this talk continues as we work through a cycle of assessment, demonstration, practice with support, independent practice, and back to assessment. The structure of the workshop is ideally suited for implementing this cycle. We use the workshop model across the curriculum.

Workshops

WRITING WORKSHOP

These children do not profit from being taken away from the rich language of a reading or a writing workshop in order to work on discrete, out-of-context skills. It is a terrible mistake for an English language learner to practice in the hall with an ELL teacher using flashcards containing colors or seasons while his or her classmates tell and write stories, make explanations, describe, question, reminisce, revise, amplify, clarify, and reach for words to convey meanings.

Lucy Calkins, *Units of Study for Primary Writing: A Yearlong Curriculum*

It had been very hot that day in late September, and the first graders were relieved to get back to the cool classroom. Everyone was exhausted after our first field trip. The children had been so excited. Many of them rarely leave the Spanish-speaking community centered in the apartments near our school, so today had been a grand adventure! They had waded through long grass, picked apples from high up in the trees, ridden on a wagon behind a tractor, examined crops in the fields, clucked at the chickens, waved handfuls of grass at the horses, and selected their very own pumpkin from the huge pile at the entrance to the farm. After visiting the apple orchard and organic farm, the excitement continued at a playground in a woodland park, where we had a picnic and some serious playtime.

For some of our newer ELLs, the strain of trying to make sense out of this barrage of new experiences and the related onslaught of teacher talk had left them in a state of total exhaustion. Hot, tired little bodies slumped against each other and nodded off as soon as the bus pulled out onto the road for the drive home. The teachers were worn out too!

Arriving back at the classroom, Emelie put on some soft music and told the children they could rest, paint with water colors, read, play puzzles, go to the listening center, draw, or do any quiet activity they could think of. You get the picture. Emelie just wanted to sit in the rocking chair and drink water. Dismissal began before they knew it. "But we haven't had writing workshop. We can't go home yet!" complained the children.

How do we get the children to love writing workshop so much that by the end of September they already miss it when it is cut out of their day, or in the spring, they groan if we have to cut off their writing time at an hour? How does this happen? How do we explain it to others? We began to think of the many visitors who have observed in our rooms over the years. What questions have they asked most often?

Responding to these questions will help us paint a picture of how this passion develops in young writers who are just learning English. Many of our kindergarten students and older newcomers come with no knowledge of the alphabet. However, we start writing workshop the first day and model how we expect them to participate as writers. We offer as many authentic writing experiences as possible and provide as much encouragement as needed to work at these tasks.

We keep the second language learner in our minds as we plan daily a writing workshop that encourages and allows for group talk during story time, writing time, and sharing time. We develop a format that provides children opportunities to have one-on-one time with an adult who listens to their oral descriptions of their pictures and helps them as they learn to write letters, sounds, and words. All of this individual time, individual talk, and individual teaching challenges the second language learners to grow as writers as they are learning to speak and read English.

The First Days of Writing Workshop

In Emelie's class, some of the first-day jitters had subsided for both students and teacher by the time of the first writing workshop. Children had looked for names on the cards laid out on the floor. Eleven of the children were able to recognize their names and bring Emelie their cards. A volunteer had snapped a photo of each child with a digital camera so they could start matching names to pictures the second day. To help learn names, the students had sung and danced to personalized versions of *Mary Wore Her Red Dress and Henry Wore His Green Sneakers* by Merle Peck. "Melvin wore his blue shirt, blue shirt, blue shirt. Melvin wore his blue shirt all day long." Emelie had learned the children's names and hoped her pronunciations were right.

Now it was time for the first whole-group lesson of the year. Emelie looked at the students watching her carefully. A few looked comfortable, some looked nervous, and some looked downright scared. The languages they spoke were Spanish, Arabic, Urdu, Bangla, Somali, Vietnamese, Chinese, and English. She took a deep breath and jumped in.

"This is my favorite part of the school day. I miss this time of day in the summer. You had this time every day in kindergarten. Now you will have it in first, second, third, fourth, and fifth grade. And pretty much you are the boss of this part of the day. It is called writing workshop." With this whispered announcement, writing workshop had begun for another year.

The first day, the first week, and maybe the first few weeks our main goals during writing workshop are making each child feel secure as a writer while establishing the routines and rituals of writing workshop. We keep the routine very simple. The basic format will remain the same all year. At the beginning of the year, the time spent with the teacher modeling writing is longer, and the child's writing time is short. This ratio gradually changes.

While in our circle, we read a story and we talk about it, have a short mini-lesson, and engage the children in the writing process as we model writing for them. Each child decides on his or her own topic and goes off to write. The teacher's job these first weeks is to walk around and assist children while they are writing. The first day, the child's time with pencil in hand writing may be only ten minutes, but the time will lengthen daily. The children come back to the circle to share their writing. We put closure on the workshop by saying what we noticed them doing well and give a hint of what we will teach the next day. We establish routines they can come to rely on throughout the year. There is a double purpose for spending days helping everyone understand the routine. It establishes behavioral expectations so children can work independently, which will free up the teacher to confer with students.

The books we choose these first days and weeks will introduce children to different types of writing: books that have photographs or illustrations with no text, books with labels or short phrases for text, bilingual books, nonfiction books, simple storybooks, realistic fiction, and fantasy. We explicitly tell them the names of the genre as we read the books. We are communicating to the children that they may write in many different ways and that we are going to accept their topic choices and attempts.

The mini-lessons in September are about topic choice as well as work-shop routine: where the different papers are stored and which ones you can choose, why we do not sharpen our pencils during writing workshop, why we put dates on writing. Because we do not assign topics during writing work-shop, topic choice is a mini-lesson that we revisit throughout the year. We often look at where authors in the classroom and outside the classroom get their ideas. We start our first ongoing chart together this week. The title is "What Writers Write About." We begin our list of topics: racecars, Mom, Dad, dinosaurs, soccer, school.

It is often hard work to keep everyone engaged during these first days of writing workshop, as we sit in the circle listening to the story and thinking about our writing work. As we teach, we try to assess how much English our students have and give everyone opportunities to talk about familiar sub-jects. Some students are not prepared to take any risks yet to help us figure this out. Each circle time is an exhausting balancing act between teaching, assessing, nurturing, and reengaging. In addition, some children need more help than others to stay engaged.

During one of these first lessons in Emelie's kindergarten class, Jesse acts as though he has ants in his pants. Mohammad wants to chatter in Arabic to his best friend. Jebin's straight face isn't giving Emelie many clues to what she is thinking. Ana still looks shell-shocked. Emelie thinks Ana's state is a combination of being separated from her twin, Jasmin, and the "noise" of all the English. Emelie pats the floor next to her, smiles, and slips her arm around Ana. Ana snuggles up next to Emelie. Emelie feels Ana's body relax as she continues with her lesson.

Before the children can go off to write, Emelie chooses a large sheet of paper. She asks them to listen as she thinks aloud. "Today I think I'll write on this paper with no lines on it because I want to draw a big picture of me on a boat at the pond." Noticing Mohammad is wiggling over to grasp the blocks, Emelie engages him with, *"Mohammad, will you come up here and hold these markers for me? Thank you. Now I think I'll write the names of my* grandchildren next to their pictures because you don't know them, and I want you to know who they are. I'll label this *Emelie*. She is the oldest. She is six. Then there is Mark and Travis and Jonathan and Kristen and little Parker. We are all in the boat together. *Jesse, would you count how many people are in the boat? Thank you, there are seven people in the boat."*

Emelie says, "Now I need to write a story. I think I'll write the words down here near the bottom of the paper. I want you to know we caught some fish. I'll start my story. 'We went fishing. We got a little fish and a big fish.' Jebin, what's this? That's right, it's a fish. Did you ever catch a fish?" Jebin shakes her head no, and Emelie makes a mental note that Jebin has some receptive language. After the children watch her write, Emelie dismisses them to begin drawing and writing just as she had modeled for them. *"Jesse, if you are ready, go and choose your paper from the writing center first."* (Every day that week the class will be involved in shared writing where they will help Emelie make decisions about the selection of paper types, topics, pictures, and text.)

As the children in all classrooms write, teachers move from table to table chatting briefly with each child, letting them know that they are telling information through their art, their scribbles, their misspellings, or any attempts they make. We encourage the children to have conversations at their tables about the pictures they are drawing and explain that the stories are in their heads and others want to know them. These little conferences that start in September are precious snippets of time for a teacher to give a child his or her undivided attention.

As the children are working daily in writing workshops across the primary grades, teachers are busy supporting all students with the tasks of holding pencils, erasing, drawing, organizing, folding paper, stapling, finding where to start, spelling, thinking of the right word, and all the other complicated tasks involved in writing. As we walk around, we are finding out useful information about each student that we draw on later to develop whole-group, small-group, and individual mini-lessons.

We set expectations that we know students can meet those first days. We make sure they are successful as writers. Every day the students tell stories, draw pictures, write, and share pieces. We try to get to as many children as possible with brief comments and conversations to show we care about their writing. Our teaching points show the children we see them as writers by telling them that they are doing what writers do: telling stories through art, labeling with letters, writing words or sentences. To give students the language of writer's craft we might say, "The beginning of your story makes me want to know more. We call the beginning of your story a lead. It leads us to the rest of the story. Class! Listen to this lead, 'My Mom went to the hospital.' Doesn't it make us want to know more about his Mom?"

61

Again, let's join Emelie's class that first week as she informally confers with each small group of writers. She sits down with the group working at one table.

"Jebin, you know how to write your name. We want everyone to know who wrote this. Where can you write your name?

"Mishaal, you know that illustrators put lots of details in their pictures. I see your Mom here. Where is she? OK, Mom's at home. How can you show us that in your picture?

"Jesse, you know that writers put words on their paper that go with their pictures. Tell me what else you are going to write about this picture."

Emelie turns to Ana. "Ana, is this you in the picture? Let's put your name here." Emelie takes her hand and gently helps her write the A in the air. Emelie points to the A on the alphabet strip saying, "You write the A, and I'll write the rest. This is the sun. Can you say 'sun'? Good. I'll write *sun* here. What is this? Yes, it's the sun."

Those first days there is time for extensive sharing because their stamina for writing is not very long. The children show what they have done. As they share, we start modeling how to listen for understanding. We let the students know that we expect them to try their best to understand what their friends are communicating through their sharing. Children present their writing, and we model questions, comments, and suggestions. At the beginning of the year their writing is so short that all may share. However, as the year goes on and their writing becomes longer, children may share with a few friends in a small group or share just a portion of their writing with the whole class.

The following comments and questions are from a closing of one of Emelie's first writing workshops. "Thank you for sharing your writing today. I have something for you to think about. What went well for you during writing workshop? What did you do that writers do? What did you see someone else do that writers do?"

Often dead silence will meet these questions at the beginning of the year. However, we know that gradually the children will learn to talk about their writing. We tell the students some of the things that we saw them do as writers. We might read from some of our anecdotal notes to show that what they did was important enough to write down. "You already know some things that writers do. Tomorrow I will plan a lesson to teach you something new that writers do. Today Joel wrote about snakes. Writers write about what they know. Joel may be our class expert on snakes. I know all of you are experts on something. When you are an expert on something, you can write a special kind of book about it. Think about it tonight. What are you an expert on? Tomorrow I'll show you how to do that kind of writing. Every day we will learn new things to make you a better writer."

Meeting a Wide Range of Needs Through Writing Workshop Structure

Writing workshop enables the teacher to meet the needs of all the children. We always want to remain aware that each child in the class deserves our best teaching as well as thoughtful planning for what they need next in their learning. We choose our books, mini-lessons, and teaching points with care.

During writing workshop we are able to teach various genres, including nonfiction, letter writing, and poetry. By doing so, we can meet the needs of all the children in our class. We can suggest to Joel that he might want to learn to write a nonfiction piece on snakes, or children can learn to write letters home or to the principal. When Trini had a terrible case of poison ivy, the class had been in the midst of a poetry unit. She used poison ivy as her topic and for several days revised her poem. (See Figure 4.1.)

Poison Ivy
Poison ivy on my neck
Poison ivy on my leg
Poison ivy on my hand
And I don't like it.

Poison ivy on my finger
Poison ivy on my side
Poison ivy on my ear
Yucky, yucky, yucky

Poison ivy on my other hand
Poison ivy on my cheek
Poison ivy everywhere
And I hate it.
By Trini

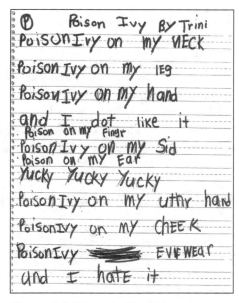

Figure 4.1 "Poison Ivy" by Trini.

Choosing a Topic

First, we must be clear that we do not tell children what to write. In an article in the November 2004 *Language Arts*, Donald Graves looks at what remains the same over twenty years of teaching writing. The first point he lists affirms our practice of children, not teachers, selecting the topics. "Children need to choose most of their own topics. But we need to show them all the places writing comes from, that it is often triggered by simple everyday events." Sometimes we do assign writing topics but not during writing workshop. At other workshops children may be asked to write on a specific topic: a reader's response, a math word problem, about an experiment, or what they are learning in a content area. The following story illustrates the importance of teaching children how to choose a topic.

We had all arrived back at school after our spring break and were chatting excitedly upon seeing each other again. Finally, after an extended time talking together, we got around to our greeting routine and sharing our morning stories. The children happily greeted each other one at a time all around the circle. The greetings finally reached José. He had held his story in all morning, waiting for this moment to share his big news.

"Good morning, José."

"Good morning, Mishaal. I have something to share."

"Do you want to share it?"

"Yes, please. My mother had a baby. His name is Matthew David. He is cute. He cries."

The other children peppered him with questions, and he was thrilled. The baby had come at the beginning of spring break. He had been waiting for nine days to say the words, "I have something to share." He held the story in, knowing that there was a time when he would be able to share. During writing time, he wrote a story he must have been rehearsing for nine days as well.

José showed us how much he depended on this established routine. He had chosen a topic for his first day back after spring break and knew there would be time to share it, both orally and in writing.

Mini-Lessons as Part of the Structure

Throughout the year the structure stays the same as everyone gathers on the floor at the beginning of the workshop and at the end, to celebrate our day's writing. What we choose to read and discuss as a springboard for the mini-lesson changes: a book, a poem, our own writing, or a child's writing. The technique to teach the mini-lesson often changes also, based on the needs of the children. It could be the teacher thinking out loud, voicing her thought process as she writes a short story. It might be children and teacher sharing the marker and writing together. Or the teacher might use a child's piece of writing to teach a certain skill. Perhaps the teacher will refer to and reread parts of a favorite mentor book to demonstrate something the author did that the children might try. Occasionally we use this time to teach a literary convention or revisit a workshop routine. The important thing is that a mini-lesson should include the ELLs, whether the lesson is on expectations for behaviors while writing, choosing a topic, or the writer's craft.

One way we include the ELLs is to make overheads of their writing to use as a mini-lesson. We might say, "Today we are going to learn from Ali. Let's look at Ali's writing and see what he did that writers do. What do you notice?"

We work to make choosing a writing topic easy for all our students, understanding that our ELLs might need extra support. One way is to make the lesson more concrete. For example, when we teach how writers choose topics, we describe our personal stories as coming from our hearts or our heads.

One day after the first graders had shared their stories orally in the circle, Tess put up a big piece of chart paper. She divided it into a T-chart. At the top of the left side she drew a heart. At the top of the right side she drew a head. Then she turned to Jorge.

Tess: Jorge, tell me what your story was about today.
Jorge: It was about my new baby.
Tess: Why did you tell us about your baby sister?
Jorge: Because I love her.
Tess: That's right. You do. Do you think that would be a story from your heart or from your head? Which side of the chart shall I write that on?
Jorge: By the heart.

Tess continued to add the topics generated by that morning's discussion to the appropriate side of the chart. The students were able to refer to this growing list over the next weeks whenever anyone was stumped for a writing topic.

We look for chances to bring our English language learners' stories to the forefront as topics by reading their body language: looking for new clothes, new hair cuts, lost teeth, new babies being born, found items from the playground. These are all rich writing topics that are important to our children.

Another way we get children to share the narrative in their lives is to talk about how writers write about what they do, people and things they know, and places they go. We make a chart to record story topics and let the children add to it as they tell or write stories from their lives.

This type of topic chart has three labeled columns under the heading Writers Write About: Things They Do, People and Things They Know, and Places They Go. Children begin to realize that playing soccer, digging a garden, going to McDonald's, learning about dinosaurs, making tortillas, or cleaning houses with Mom are all topics for stories to tell and write. Through this process, children are learning how their stories are important and unique. What they know is different from what other people know and worthy to be shared. They learn they are experts in areas different from their friends. We soon find out who knows about dinosaurs, who knows the rules of soccer, who knows the parts of insects, and who is an expert on cooking. Children thus learn that their stories have an audience. They learn they are sharing knowledge and events through their writing.

These story-topic lessons are short and for the whole class. We want the lessons to be quick so that the children can use most of the writing workshop time for independent writing. Often the mini-lessons at the beginning of writing workshop will focus on ways to write about the different topics. We teach how to write nonfiction books, how to label diagrams, how to add dialog, and so on.

One way to keep the momentum of the writing lesson going is to have the students tell the class or tell partners what they plan to write that day. Emelie often asks the students to take a moment to think about their plans. She then says, "Who knows what they will write about?" A few hands shoot up. Emelie calls on Trini. "My Grandma!" Trini exclaims. Emelie says, "Great, go for it! Who else?"

As Emelie calls on students, she makes a mental note of each topic and, when done, enthusiastically responds, "Great! Go." Students tell the others what they will be writing about that day as they leave the circle: "I'm going to write about my baby." "I'm going to write more on my playground story." "I'm going to finish drawing about whales." "Race cars!" "Rainbows!" "Flowers!" We do this as efficiently as possible so that children can get to their writing and write for an extended period. Some students have come to school that morning with their topic already planned. Others might need a little prompting before they decide on a topic. And one or two might need to stay behind for a little one-on-one support in selecting a topic. This is a good time for Emelie to engage in a quick conversation. "Hey Carlos, I noticed you have a new haircut. Tell me about it."

Art is another way we tell our stories. Every day we give the children the opportunity to draw their stories before they write. As the children draw, they are encouraged to talk to each other about their artwork. Their questions and comments generate more details to add to their drawings. Language flows during writing time. Their artwork becomes the topic. Oral language during writing time helps develop the writing and the development of English. It helps with the composing and constructing of the written story.

In their book *Reading, Writing, & Learning in ESL* Peregoy and Boyle say that

> all students bring rich personal experiences in the classroom. If they are given the opportunities to voice these experiences orally and in writing, you will find that they will always have valid topics to write about and plenty to say. . . . The process approach to writing is espe-

cially valuable for English learners because it allows them to write from their own experiences. (1997, p. 191)

Many times we have watched our colleague Kathleen Fay confer with children at every grade level. It is as if she can see into their memories. She is able to pull "stuff" out of children, reminding them of this, that, or the other thing during the day and during writing workshop. Kathleen says that "a good teacher acts as the child's memory, scaffolding and showing them how to bring bits of their lives into the workshop."

As the children are writing, we move from student to student, conferring with as many children as we can during the workshop. Our interest in their topic will lead to a child having confidence in his or her ability to choose topics. We tell them what we see them doing well as writers. "Haider, I notice you are writing about your trip to Pakistan today. You are doing what writers do. You are writing about a place you went to and things you learned. I couldn't write about Pakistan. I have never been there or eaten their delicious food. I can't even speak the languages of Pakistan. You are the expert on Pakistan in this class." We tell children what they are doing well as writers to make it explicit to them. We want the children to do it later in another piece. The students need to be able to identify the actual writing behavior or process so that they will begin to internalize the abstract and complex aspects of writing.

Occasionally during these individual conferences we see an opportunity to extend learning by working on one teaching point from a child's piece. For example, "Jebin, you said your brother screamed. I can see on your face how he looked! Oh, my! Let me show you how to write what your brother screamed so the reader can feel like he's here." Often when we are conferring with one child, the other children at the table are listening. They share in the learning. Writing conferences can provide the content of follow-up focus lessons, as we learn what the students need. An overhead made of Jebin's writing could be used to teach a whole-group focus lesson the following day on using exclamation points.

During sharing time at the end of writing workshop, children will pick up an idea for the next day's topic. Listening to a friend share about the topic "all about frogs" will give them confidence to choose "all about volcanoes" the next day.

Tess and Emelie have each spent time as writing teachers for upper-grade English language learners. It is exciting to see how both the mini-lessons and conferring times parallel the ones from the primary grades. Older children experience more in-depth lessons and more time spent with the pen to become more proficient at "doing what writers do" than the primary children. However, lessons on leads, using strong verbs, and giving mind pictures to your audience are useful for both kindergarten students and fifth graders. These young second language learners who are making their first attempts to offer their comments, questions, and suggestions will become increasingly proficient as writers as they read, listen, and discuss hundreds of books, pieces of writing, and what "writers do" year after year.

Helping Children Write English in the Beginning Stages of Literacy

It was writing workshop during February in Carrie Omps's first-grade classroom. A new student, Carla, had arrived from El Salvador the week before and spoke no English. Carla had been in school in El Salvador, so she was reading and writing in Spanish. As the class began writing workshop, Carrie encouraged Carla to write her story in Spanish. When she met with Carla to discuss her writing, Carrie quietly called Kelly over to join them. Kelly, a Spanish speaker, spoke English well enough to translate for Carla and had taken Carla under her wing since the day she arrived.

Carla read her story in Spanish with Kelly translating. Carrie praised the girl for writing such an interesting story. Kelly then repeated this in Spanish to Carla, who looked very pleased with herself. With Kelly's help, Carrie enabled Carla to share her writing. Carla was not quite ready to share in front of the whole class, but, being a risk taker, it will not be long before she has the confidence to give it a try.

Carla is literate in her own language. What a bonus! She knows about telling stories in writing, about letters and words and sound-symbol relationships, and about using resources in the room to problem-solve. Her skills will soon transfer over into her new language. In the meantime, she is able to participate as much as possible in Spanish in her new school community, and since her efforts are valued, she will soon develop the confidence needed to take risks in English.

Many of the children in our classrooms, however, have much less experience with literacy than Carla. These children also participate fully in writing workshop. Some children have never held a pencil or crayon and may need lots of practice making marks and drawing letter-like forms on dry-erase boards and scratch paper before they are ready to write letters. We give them clay to develop their hand muscles. As they use these tools, they are again surrounded by language. As they draw, paint, or make sculptures with clay, the students are engaged in conversation by teachers and friends. They are engaged by listening to caring adults and kind peers who use invented sign language, visuals, and props. These ELLs are given repeated demonstrations and are held responsible for making some decisions. The teachers have high expectations for their abilities and accept their approximations. Children have many opportunities to hear teachers respond in ways that both support each child individually and teach each child appropriate next steps.

We are striving to implement Brian Cambourne's conditions for learning in a safe place where children can take risks in both oral and written language. So much of a workshop is oral language, and Cambourne says that "while the conditions for learning to talk cannot be precisely replicated for the written mode of language, the principles which they exemplify can." He goes on to say that "when teachers understand the principles they can and do arrange their classrooms so that they simulate for the written form of the language what the world appears to do naturally for the oral form. When they do this, the learning which occurs is both powerful and durable" (1988).

We know that the children's early pictures tell their stories until they learn to produce the words that go with the story in English orally and later in writing. Often their pictures are of things dear to their hearts or in their everyday lives. Their first English words often grow from these pictures: *Mom, soccer, race car, house, sun.* Soon they will start labeling their pictures and then move on to writing full sentences.

As with any emergent writers, ELLs who have not yet learned literacy skills in their own language begin at the beginning. Some might start with printlike scribble, strings of random letters, or the alphabet. Others might be ready to start applying what they know about sound-symbol relationships and write beginning or ending sounds that they hear in words as they say them. Children need lots of help with sounds and letters when they are writing. We share the pen, allowing the child to write known sounds and words while we quickly fill in what he or she does not know. (See Figure 4.2.) More information on sharing the pen with young writers is available in the book *Interactive Writing* (McCarrier, Pinnell, and Fountas).

We also help the children by providing alphabet strips, high-frequency words taped to their tables or writing folders, word walls, and books in accessible places around the room. We support the children by using prompts that encourage them to think about how a word looks and sounds.

- Where have you seen that word?
- Listen for the sound.
- Say it again.
- Write the sound you hear.
- What else do you hear?

Over the years, we have learned that children can become dependent on our support for spelling. They want us to say the word slowly for them. If we say *rainbow* slowly, then they can hear most of the sounds. However, we want

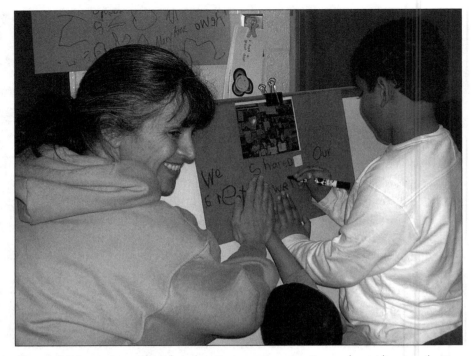

Figure 4.2 Interactive writing (shared pen) supports young writers and provides an authentic opportunity to teach what each writer needs to learn next.

them to move to independence in writing as quickly as possible. To help them, we consistently encourage children to say the words to themselves.

Teacher: You want to write *rainbow*. Say it.
Child: [silence]
Teacher: Say it with me. Rainbow.
Child with teacher: Rainbow.
Teacher: Now you say it.
Child: It.
Teacher [laughing]: Slowly, you say rainbow.
Child: R a i n b o w.
Teacher: That's great, you did it. Say it again slowly. What do you hear first? Write it. Now what do you hear next? Write that. What else do you hear? Write the sound you hear.

Raising Expectations for Young Writers

After children learn to label their pictures with a few words, we quickly raise the bar and support them in writing simple sentences. We might say, "What do you want to say?" If they say, "I like my mom," that is great. We let them write that for a couple of days and then raise the bar to "I like my mom because _____." Next, we might encourage them to add to their story by telling who else is in their family and why they like them. We might ask them to tell something they do with their mom. We are explicitly phrasing our questions and comments in a way to elicit narratives from children, even if they have only drawn pictures. Our goal is to elicit narratives; we want the students to grow from their first attempts of labels or one-word responses.

To elicit verbal narratives, we might respond to their art with the following:

- Tell me more about your picture.
- What happened next?
- Then what did you do?
- What did your mom say?

Prompts like these will peel back the layers until the real story comes out.

Students copy words from books as well as words from around the room, so lots of labels, charts, and a word wall support them. (See Figure 4.3.) Often pictures are next to the words so they can find the correct word. One way we have found to make our word wall interactive is to put words on index cards backed with pieces of magnetic tape and place them on the chalkboard under the appropriate alphabet letter. Children can remove a word to copy it and then pass it to a friend or replace it. At other times, they can take all the words off and then reorder them.

Often we will help a student write a word on the index card so he or she becomes the expert on that word, and then we can refer anyone else who needs that word to the student. "Jorge, if you need the word *like*, ask Mirla. She knows where it is." The more they see themselves as resources for each other, the more independent they become, allowing the teacher a few extra precious moments for one-on-one teaching time. To make children more independent, we put pictures on labels, signs, charts, messages, and stories. Without the pictures, the text has little or no meaning to emergent readers and writers.

Allowing students to copy text can be a way of supporting their writing development in the early stages of acquiring English. Even when they know very little receptive English they love to mimic what is going on around them. They play teacher and copy the morning message or some of the words from it. They copy the morning's shared writing that grew out of the focus lesson. They copy their friends' writing. They copy from the word wall and other resources around the room. They copy from books. As young children learn to play soccer by imitating soccer players, young writers often learn by

Figure 4.3 At the beginning of the year, Michelle Gale's word wall consists only of children's names but grows gradually as she adds words that support the writers in her room.

imitating the adults around them. We accept this as a natural stage of their development, and we know it will not last long. Mimicking is a natural part of language development. We push them to the next level and continue to challenge them to use their own language. We are always providing authentic opportunities for children to develop new language, and the copying stage passes soon.

Another type of copying that children with a little more English will do is with a clipboard. Children are fascinated by what teachers write on their note-taking clipboards. At one point early this year, the children were excited about using the clipboards in the writing center. You could not walk into the room without several children asking you to sign your name on their boards, and they were all signing each other's boards.

Children paraded around asking survey questions, such as "Do you like spiders?" Yes-or-no columns gave a place for people to write their names. Since Friday is pizza day at Bailey's, a favorite clipboard survey is "Do you like pepperoni pizza? Do you like cheese pizza?" This time children write the words *yes* or *no*.

By providing all these genuine experiences, rather than meaningless worksheet tasks, we aim to move the children on as quickly as possible from the scribbling stage to the copying stage and then onto writing pattern stories.

Picture two ELLs lying on the floor with a Big Book picture dictionary in front of them. They search the dictionary for pictures of things they like and write sentences: "I like toys." "I like dogs." "I like rainbows." We nudge them to write other patterns such as "I see the house." "I see the horse." The children are sharing this work together, so they are learning oral language as well as sight words and sentence structure. Just as the children who go through the copying stage do not stay there long, children who go through the pattern stage usually move on quickly. Their writing develops to writing that is more authentic as they gain confidence and start to understand the power and fun of the pen.

Peregoy and Boyle explain the benefits of this pattern stage, or using sentence models. "Using sentence models, students begin to experiment with the sentences and learn that sentences can be organized in a variety of ways. This gives English learners confidence in their ability to learn new English sentence structures" (1997).

Students might have personal dictionaries in which to collect their own lists of words. Picture dictionaries are very helpful, and students love to lie on the floor with a Big Book dictionary to copy from. They will find pictures of things they are familiar with and draw those pictures and copy the words.

Conferring: Conversations to Support and Encourage Young Writers

During independent writing time, when the children are all sitting around their tables drawing pictures or writing, we go from table to table and have conversations with child after child. We hope the other children around us are listening in to our individual conversations.

In these conversations we offer support as needed. We accept all of their attempts as early stages of writing development, so that they believe right from the start that they are writers. Sometimes the support we offer might be a pat on the shoulder or an encouraging word. At other times we sit and chat. These informal writing conferences allow us to give individualized support to meet each student's different needs.

We show our ELLs that we can understand what they are saying in their pictures and writing. We are demonstrating that we want their friends to understand them, too. As you read the following examples of individual conferences, keep in mind that we are choosing questions and comments to elicit talk from the children. After a sufficient wait time, we may ask the question another way.

Tell me about your picture. . . . Hmm, what else are you going to put in the picture?

In this case, we are attempting to start a conversation. If the child does not respond, we might give some vocabulary to the child by labeling parts of the picture in our conversation.

Is this a slide and a swing? . . . Are you at recess or at the park with your family? . . . Tell me more.

Now we are being an interested listener and giving the child vocabulary.

I noticed you are finished with your picture. Tell me about it. . . . What words would you like to write so that your friends can know about your story? . . . Where would you start to put the words? . . . What will you put first? . . . Do you need any help from me?

In this conference, the emphasis is on engaging the child in storytelling. We know there is more to the story than they have put in the drawing and that the expectation is that they are going to continue to write the story. We offer help. If our help isn't needed, we let the child know that when we walk away, they are to continue writing. We let children know that the expectation of writing workshop is that they will write the stories they have shared orally or in their picture.

You know that sound don't you? . . . Write the letter. . . . Now say the word again. . . . What else do you hear? . . . That's right. You can use the alphabet strip to help you write that letter. Keep going, and I'll check back with you in a few minutes.

This conference is to help a child who is sitting with pencil in hand but not writing.

Hi. I noticed you were starting to draw about our field trip. Do you mind if I draw with you, and we can talk together about the trip?

It is enjoyable to pick up crayons and draw side by side with a child, chatting as you draw. This relaxing feeling is reminiscent of lying on the livingroom floor with a friend or sibling, making up stories as you drew pictures together as children. Later the child enjoys sharing, together with the teacher, to the whole class. Teaching children that their pictures tell the story is important. The others at the table always stop, watch, and listen when a teacher starts to draw. Drawing with a child is a nice way to support one who is not able to write any words yet. This conference could lead to a mini-lesson the next day for everyone. We would refer to the child's story-picture and model how all children can tell their stories through pictures.

What a lovely apple orchard you've drawn! We did have fun on our field trip, didn't we? Can you go find a book about apples and find the word apple *in it? . . . Can you copy* apple *next to the picture of your apple tree? . . . Now your friends will be able to read the word* apple. *This is called labeling. We've seen it in lots of books haven't we? . . . What else could you label in your picture?*

In this conference, we are teaching children to be resourceful and to realize that print has meaning. If children are ready to learn to label their pictures, we read books that have pictures with labels in them. We make sure children understand that they are doing what real authors do. Before we leave them, we challenge them to label some other parts of their picture.

Can you ask someone at this table to help you find that word in the room?
Some conferences are a very quick reminder that each child in the room is a resource, too, not just the teacher.

Can you two work together and fold the paper to make a book for your little sisters and brothers at home? . . . What would you like to teach them? . . . What do you know that you think they need to learn?
This conference teaches children to work together, to label, to find words in the room, to share their work, to have a purpose in writing, to talk to each other, and to practice writing. ELLs need many resources to write. They need to use each other as one of their main resources for vocabulary, meaning, and spelling.

You are stuck? Hmm, you're wondering which letter to put next aren't you? . . . Does anyone at this table know what you can try when you are stuck? . . . Yes, who can think of another way you can solve that problem?
This conference builds independence and helps the children realize that there are many others who can help them find resources so they are able to solve their writing problems on their own. We want children to learn to solve problems so that they can do it by themselves next time. Posing the question to the table as a whole will review resources that writers use when they are stuck, such as:

- Locating words on word walls;
- Asking a friend;

- Saying the word slowly;
- Thinking of another word that sounds like that word;
- Doing your best;
- Closing your eyes and thinking what the word looks like;
- Looking in the place where you've seen it before;
- Finding it in a book;
- Clapping out each syllable, then trying one part at a time;
- Spelling it with your eyes and ears (reminders of the way the word looks and sounds).

This story is really from your heart. Would you like me to publish it so that the spelling would be like the spelling in a book? . . . Who do you think would be interested in reading it? . . . Do you want me to type it on the computer in big print? . . . Or do you want me to show you how to spell it so you can copy it over correctly? . . . OK. Come with me and watch me type it. You can read it to the class. Since this is about basketball you can take it to the PE teachers, and they will put it up in the gym. I'll make you a copy to keep so you can practice reading it.

This conference will teach the students that writing is for a purpose and that writing is important. ELLs need their work published just like all other students. The act of taking their writing out of the room and going public is powerful.

Each of these conferences has a different teaching point taken from a child's writing. Most are very short. What they all have in common is they begin with the child's own writing. This is important because it allows us to start with what children know in order to take them a step further in their learning. This gentle nudging forward builds their confidence as writers, so they are willing to write more and take more risks. We think of it as conferring by nurturing and nudging.

In other words, we are always expecting each child to write a little bit better than he or she did the day before. We have high expectations for our students and hold them accountable for their previous learning. If children have shown an understanding of spaces between words, we expect them to write with spaces. Thus, at each conference we try to tell the students what we notice them doing that writers do. Then we immediately follow with one small new teaching point about writing in English. In order to know what to teach them next, we have to be careful observers of each child because every ELL is at a different place in acquisition of oral and written language.

The heart of our teaching of writing is during conference time. This individual support is crucial to our ELLs. Given time, talk, support, and practice, an ELL should master any craft or convention that we expect any other child to master. All students are on a continuum of learning.

Sharing Your Writing and Listening to Others

Just as when we are conferring, sharing time is an opportunity to show our ELLs that we can understand what they are saying in their pictures and writing. During sharing time, we work on developing trust between the author and the audience by having authentic conversations. We build a community where students know that friends are eager to hear their work and help them grow as they are learning to be writers.

In one of Emelie's classes, children with varying degrees of English acquisition get ready to share at the end of a writing workshop. As a signal to finish up writing time and convene on the carpet, Emelie begins singing a song. The children hurriedly clean up their writing materials as they join in, "The more we share together, together, together, the more we share together, the happier we'll be. We'll hear your story and my story and my story and your story. The more we share together, the happier we'll be."

Ana snuggles up close to Emelie where she feels the most comfortable. She has the least English in the class, and she knows Emelie will help her share her writing. Jovanka and Joyce sit next to each other giggling because they both wrote about the cafeteria. Mohammad and Carlos compare their latest dinosaur drawings. We sing until everyone comes to the circle. We all sit, legs crossed, with writing on the floor in front of us.

Almost everyone is eager to be the first to share his or her picture or writing. As Emelie calls on Nhi, the students gaze expectantly as she holds her journal. Her hair shields her face as she bends over her work. She points to the sticklike figures on the page and whispers, "Nhi. Mom."

The children smile with relief. They know Nhi has crossed a major hurdle, sharing as an author for the first time. Jason says, "I know where you are. You're at the park with your Mom." Nhi smiles shyly.

Bruce Lee is next and reads, "The car is fast." He looks up and asks, "Comments, questions, or suggestions?" With great importance, he calls on three of the children who are waving their hands at him. They ask: "What color is the car?" "Did it crash?" "Did it win?" Emelie thanks them for the questions and reminds Bruce Lee, "These questions are suggestions for you to give your audience a mind picture. Tomorrow maybe you will want to add to your story."

This closing ritual of writing workshop is a powerful opportunity for ELLs to develop oral language through authentic talk. To hold up a drawing for the class to see and comment on is the simplest way for ELLs to share. It

Figure 4.4 Sarah has a captive audience as she confers and shares her latest writing with Haider, Zayd, Gabriel, and Vincent.

is also an ideal time to teach students how to listen. The key to this sharing time is keeping it celebratory yet calm. The children understand that what they say in this circle is important and that what they wrote or drew during writing workshop is important. The audience response to it is equally important. As a child finishes sharing a piece and looks expectantly around the circle, hands wave. The writer listens and responds as two or three classmates make comments, ask questions, or give suggestions. Everyone gets quiet again and turns to listen as the next person reads his or her piece. This routine takes weeks to learn and a year to polish.

The closing ritual is another opportunity to revisit, reteach, or introduce something new in response to a child's writing. The following examples illustrate how teachers and children work together to understand each other as they share writing at the close of writing workshop.

Modeling How to Listen in Order to Understand

Mohammad as usual was talking about dinosaurs in his picture. The poorly formed letters *D* and *S* were near one dinosaur. The letter *T* was near a little dinosaur. Mohammad's story confused Emelie. Emelie asked several questions as he rambled on and asked him to retell parts. When his story made sense to her, she responded, "That is so interesting, and I see where you wrote 'dinosaur eats'! You were really thinking about making your story match your picture, weren't you?" The children and Mohammad were learning from her face that "What you are saying is so interesting and important to me. I want to understand your story." They were learning to listen and value the work of others because Emelie modeled that for them. Emelie also made a simple teaching point that emphasized a process that Mohammad must understand about writing. He must make his story match his picture to allow his audience to understand the story. As Mohammad gains control of more English and more writing conventions, he will gradually move to writing sentences about his picture.

From the first day of school, we model how to listen. We lean forward and ask students, "Say it again please" or "I didn't understand you. Could you say it slowly, please?" We teach the class to look at the person talking. We ask questions honestly. If we are confused, we say so. "I understand the first part but after your Dad got home and you ate soup I got confused." We model for children how to listen in order to make meaning of what is said. We teach them that we have the same expectations for all and that we will teach them how to listen.

After students share their writing, we ask the others, "Does anyone have a comment, question, or suggestion?" We teach the children what it means to make a comment, to ask a question, and to offer a suggestion. Very young children can learn to do this well. After several weeks of practice, children will finish reading their writing, look up, and say to their classmates, "Comments, questions, or suggestions?" This strategy not only gives children a focus for their listening, but also gives writers feedback about their writing. This writing workshop structure will remain the same throughout their elementary school years.

Adults in the circle (teacher, instructional assistant, volunteer) model how to question or comment. "I have a question. What did you do after you got to the park?" "I have a comment. The part about the blood on your knee gave me a good mind picture." "I have a suggestion. Tomorrow could you tell us more about what happened when you went to Pakistan. I've never been there." Over time, children begin to learn how to listen in order to understand or how to have conversations about writing. It is not surprising to hear these conversations at their tables as they are writing.

Although we accept the first "I like your story" comments, we quickly raise the bar and explain that the writer needs to hear why, and we model, "I like your story because. . . ." We are thrilled with every brave new step ELLs take in communicating with the class and immediately start asking ourselves what is the next step for these children? How soon can we nudge them towards it?

Listening to a new language can be exhausting for children who have little or no English though, and we know that sometimes they tune us out. The students can get tired, and we need to give them a rest. We expect a little rolling on the floor, fiddling with their shoes, or playing with their friend's hair during sharing time. We allow for these moments of time off task or rest from English and find ways to cue everyone back in when it is important for all to listen.

Nonverbal Sharing

If children cannot speak or write English, we celebrate that they have the courage to show their drawings to their classmates. We smile and give the children the English words for their drawings.

It is sharing time in Emelie's class, and Ana snuggles up closer and closer to Emelie. Ana knows it is going to be her turn soon. She plops the journal in Emelie's lap. Emelie gently hands it back to her. Ana holds it up for everyone to see and hides behind the picture. Emelie points to the child in the picture and says, "Ana, is that you? And is that your twin sister Jasmin?" Ana snuggles up even closer to Emelie and smiles broadly as the students raise their hands, wanting to have a turn to talk. Ana mumbles their names as she calls on them and smiles at their responses.

"I played with Jasmin at recess," sings out Joyce.

"Does Jasmin start with a J like my name?" asks José.

"I can show your how to write a J," offers Jesse, and he jumps up and runs and gets a magnetic J off the board for Ana to hold.

Scribing and Sharing for the Writer

In order for some children to share, we may offer support by acting as scribe and guest reader. At the beginning of the year, Mohammad could speak English but did not have letter or sound knowledge. Day after day, he would draw colorful dragon or dinosaur stories. As he stood at his table and drew, he entertained his tablemates for long periods of time with details, plots, and adventures that mostly only made sense to him. Of course, he wanted to share his story again during whole-group sharing time. Emelie used his strong oral language to develop his writing. Sometimes though, during writing time, Emelie would offer to help him get his story into a more comprehensible story structure.

"Would you like me to write the story the way it would look in a book for you so we can share it with the class?" As a scribe for Mohammad, Emelie helped give the story some structure as they manipulated the language together. As she read it back to him, he corrected her until it finally was the way he wanted it. At sharing time, Mohammad then chose Emelie to read his story to the class as his guest reader. "This is how my story would look in a book. Mrs. Parker will read it to you." As his writing skills increased, he started labeling *D* for *dinosaur* and eventually writing sentences.

Encouraging Children to Support One Another

We can show students how in some books the author and illustrator are not the same person. We then have children pair up as illustrators and authors to collaborate on stories. This pairing of children worked beautifully for Austin and David. They worked together to create a folded book about how to make paper boats and masks. David, a Vietnamese speaker, needed help with the English vocabulary. Austin needed help with spelling. Both were excellent artists. When they collaborated on a story, they were able to share a piece that made sense to the class. For David and Austin to be able to work together they had to engage in many complex tasks built around oral language as they planned, negotiated their writing, and decided how to share their expertise with the class.

We give children the gift of time by accepting their present stage of oral sharing just as we accept their present stage of writing development. Being able to participate fully in the sharing as Nhi, Ana, and Mohammad did, builds their confidence and allows them to learn from the other students at their own pace of language acquisition. Ana is in the silent stage, Nhi is barely emerging from the silent stage, and Mohammad's chatter is a confusing mix of languages that takes some ingenuity to decipher.

We see writing as one of the activities Virginia Collier is talking about when she says that "second language acquisition is a dynamic, creative, innate process, best developed through contextual, meaningful activities that focus on language use, combined with guidance along the way from the teacher that sometimes involves a focus on language form" (1995).

When a child holds up a picture, makes up a story, and pretends to read, that is progress. When a child has one word written on a page and "reads" a long sentence or has one sentence on a page and "reads" a whole story, we need to celebrate that the child understands that a complete story is in his or her piece. We accept these early developmental stages of writing or reading, and we rejoice in the fact that the children are seeing themselves as writers. Over and over in the classroom, children are rewarded with a spontaneous ovation from their classmates when they realize that a child has made a breakthrough. In the sharing circle, many times children will make eye contact with the teacher and give us that grown-up smile that says, "Look what he did! Aren't we proud of him? He is learning!"

Community and Closure

Sharing time is brought to a close with a succinct review and clear example of a lesson. We keep the children involved and use their work. We use English language learners' work as often as we use other students' work. It is one part of sharing closure time when we cue everyone back in to listen. We want children to know that they are equal members of our writing workshop.

In Emelie's room, the class knows to listen when Mrs. Parker chants, "Time to teach, time to teach." Right after sharing you might hear her chant: "Time to teach. Time to teach. Time for Mrs. Parker to teach." The children know this is important, and everyone sits up and gets in the "listening position." They are ready to "listen with their ears and eyes." During this quick review, we might:

- Use students' pieces from the day's workshop and show them to the class. We tell the class we will talk more about this tomorrow. For example, "Donte got stuck today when he ran out of space on the page when he was writing. Look what he did to solve the problem. Tomorrow we will talk about more ways to solve this problem."
- We make charts with the children and leave them up, adding to them as needed. "Today I noticed that Jesse, Cindy, and Josue used strong verbs in their stories. Let's make a chart and keep a list of the strong verbs we use. Jesse, come write your name and put *charge* next to it. Then Cindy, you can put your name and *leaped* next to yours. Tomorrow we will talk some more about why authors use strong verbs in their writing." We make charts *with* the children, not before class, and we draw pictures on the charts together so that everyone can refer to them. We add to them slowly, day by day, and only as information comes up. We refer to them as we teach and as the children use them in their writing.
- We celebrate growth. "Let's show Mohammad one more time how proud we are of him because he knows that the words have to match his pictures. We are so glad he knows what writers do. He wrote a sentence today that went with his pictures. Look, Mohammad, it is on our chart titled What Do Writers Do? Writers write about their pictures. You did that today. You are a writer!"
- We review the mini-lesson and ask students who may have tried out what we talked about earlier to show us examples. "Who can show us where they used a strong word?"

This closure time at the end of writing workshop is important. It builds community. It gives story ideas to other students, develops language, and gives a purpose for writing. It teaches children how to read their own work to an audience and how to listen and comment on each other's writing. It teaches them how to ask questions, how to write for others, and how to think about their audience. The closing routine and the rituals that go with it are also important because they are fun.

Building Stamina for Writing

"Teacher, I'm done!" Haven't we all heard that over and over in our classrooms? We have to have an answer for children as they are building their stamina during writing workshop time. The answer is, "Writing workshop is never finished. It continues all the way until the end of your life. You are always writing. If you have talked with an adult about today's writing, it's time for you to make a choice of what other writing work to do." We have already introduced and explained these choices during the mini-lessons in the first month of school when the class was learning the routine of writing workshop.

Writing work can be any of many literacy activities. We encourage the children to do work that will make them better writers. It is true that some ELLs do not have the stamina or enough skills to continue writing for an hour or an hour and a half, so we provide choices for them. If they have finished their drawing and writing for the day and have worked with an adult, the students then choose an activity including, but not limited to:

- Reading books in the class library or at listening centers
- Playing ABC puzzles or games
- Exploring reading-and-writing-based software
- Writing words or letters on dry-erase boards
- Manipulating magnetic letters
- Matching names of classmates to photos
- Writing with clipboards
- Writing at tables in the writing centers
- Folding paper into books
- Writing cards for friends
- Writing signs for the room
- Drafting on the computer

These are all independent activities that the teacher explains and models. The activities encourage talk while giving children opportunities to do more reading and writing at their own level. These social activities involve conversation and sharing, which give the ELLs more opportunities to experiment with English in nonthreatening situations. Needless to say, the classroom hums with conversation at this time of the day. The children and the

83

teacher work out what the acceptable noise level is for the workshop. Children group and regroup as they move fluidly between the learning activities, enabling our ELLs to interact with children speaking differing levels of English. The teacher then has the opportunity to work one-on-one with the other children who are still writing their pieces. When the students hear the song signaling time to come to the sharing circle, they quickly put away their writing work, gather their journals or writing workshop pieces, and come to the circle. We have designed the workshop to engage students the entire time in work that will help them become more skillful writers.

Using Assessment as a Tool for Teaching

At the end of the school year, Emelie finished writing all the progress reports, started on the cumulative records, and filed the portfolios for the next year's teachers. In celebration, she didn't bother to take notes during her writing conference with Hamdiya. After putting her book box and journal away, Hamdiya started reading poems on the overhead projector. Then out of the corner of her eye, Emelie saw the girl dash back to her cubby. She came flying over to Emelie with her well-worn, year-old, ongoing assessment card that is kept in her book box. "Here Mrs. Parker, you forgot to write down what smart thing I did today and what new thing you taught me!"

To know what to teach next we have to know what each child can do now. This takes the form of ongoing assessment. It begins at open house before school starts, as families come to school to meet the teacher and see where the room is. Emelie asks her kindergarteners to sign in on open-house day and during the first weeks of school. This provides one of her early opportunities for assessment. How do the children control the task of holding the pen? Do they control letter formation? Do they use upper- or lower-case letters or a mix? Do they control directionality? Do they know the letters of their name? If they are unable to write their name, can they find it on a list? Ongoing assessment is a type of assessment we all strive to perfect, but it is so hard to do with a room full of active children.

As we observe, we notice there are items we need to address with the whole group and others that only a small group needs to learn. Some items will have to be addressed one-on-one. We will have to clarify certain points, reteach items, build on what is known, or teach a needed skill. Each child has a different subset of skills and knowledge of writing. We have to be watching everyone all day every day. We see glimpses of literate moments in math and walking down the hall, and we see snippets of literacy during shared writing and again at recess. Throughout writing workshop we watch and try to hold it all in our heads. We try to remember who knows what. It seems impossible. On sticky notes, file cards, check lists, notebooks, or folders, we jot down what we see.

There are many ways to keep records. Teachers love to play around with different ones, searching for the one that is the most user-friendly. Here is one system Emelie devised that works for her during writing workshop. She places colorful cards made of card stock in the children's book boxes where they keep their journals and writing supplies. When she sits down to confer with them, she can quickly look at the cards and see what they worked on together at the last writing conference, what sounds the children know, what words they can spell, and what skills and strategies have been talked about in the past. These records help Emelie hold the children accountable for their knowledge.

On the front of the card is the alphabet in both upper-case and lower-case letters. As the children learn to name the letters, Emelie simply underlines each one that they know and can then hold the children responsible for knowing those letters.

As she notices they are connecting a sound with the correct letter in their writing, she highlights it. Emelie can then expect the students to use those sounds in their writing. When a child wants to write *soccer*, Emelie can take a quick glance at the card and notice that the *s* is highlighted. She can say, "You know that sound. What sound do you hear when you say soccer? Can you write what you hear?"

On the back of the cards, Emelie lists known words that the children can spell. As they learn to spell words such as *mom, the, like*, she adds them to the list. When she is writing with a child, she can glance at the card and use this to help her know what to teach. She might say, "You know how to write *we*. How can writing *we* help you write *me?*"

Stapled to this assessment card is a blank piece of paper where Emelie writes very short notes about the conference each day. Here are some examples of notes from different children's cards (*P* = prompt, *TP* = teaching point):

- *Jesse 9–18 P–spaces TP–books*. Jesse needed to use spaces between words. Emelie asked him to show her where an author used spaces in a book so Jesse could do the same thing.
- *Barivure 9–19 P–used details. TP–add dets to pics so can add dets to story tomorrow Go to mult.sents*. Emelie asked Barivure to add more details to his pictures, which, in turn, would create more details he could add to the text of his story the next day. She noted that he is ready to write multiple sentences in his stories. She will think about who else can join him for a mini-lesson on extending stories.

- *Jerry 10–24 Told long story with b, m, e.* Jerry told Emelie an involved story with a beginning, a middle, and an end. She thought that by modeling his story during shared writing, it would help motivate him to try writing a three-part story on his own. Several other students were ready for this too.

- *Ythrip 11–7 Indep.1st time!!! . I wnt (went) to my ks/cousins hs/house. TP–WROTE BY SELF> Tom. Add what did at cousins.* Emelie celebrated Ythrip's first independently written story. She let Ythrip know how interested she was to find out what Ythrip and her cousin did together. Tomorrow she planned to remind Ythrip to write about that because everyone would want to know.

From her notes on the cards, Emelie can plan to pull out children for direct teaching on spaces between words, or she can plan to teach mini-lessons on writing a beginning, a middle, and an end and adding details to stories to create mind pictures for audiences. She can take a group of students who are each attempting the word *went* in different ways (*wt, wnt, whet, wnet*) in their writing and teach them to spell it correctly. By looking at these notes to assess student needs, she is able to see which craft or convention she can teach that would help them become better writers.

Tess keeps similar notes, but she uses a sheet marked into a grid on a clipboard. There is a square labeled for each child in the class. The notes she records are very similar to those described in Emelie's record-keeping. Down the right-hand side of the sheet is a blank column, where Tess keeps an ongoing list of lessons she needs to teach. She records whether it needs to be a whole-group lesson, a small-group lesson, or an individual one. When she gives the lesson, she records the date of it and has a record of what, who, and when she taught.

These kinds of notes help guide our instruction for each child in our daily conferences. They help us teach within the child's zone of proximal development and keep us from expecting too much or too little of each child.

There is such a range of ability in any class, especially when you have ELLs in your room. Such notes show us that we cannot meet the needs of each child by delivering only whole-group instruction. We must also plan for small-group instruction and one-on-one instruction, in addition to the mini-lessons we plan for the whole class. When we confer with parents or when we need to look to see how a child is progressing over time, these records are invaluable.

No matter how we record or organize them, notes help guide our instruction for each child in our daily conferences. We write abbreviated shorthand, and fast. We just want to get enough down so we can read it later to plan. Tess keeps her clipboard by her side as she confers with students but sometimes resorts to scribbling notes on computer labels, sticky notes, or scraps of paper.

These notes keep us from expecting too much or too little from each child. Several years ago our school spent a year learning to understand Vygotsky's (1978) theory of the zone of proximal development and to apply this thinking to each student's learning. Reflecting on notes helps to ensure that we are teaching each child at the appropriate instructional level. The instructional level is where a child can perform with help. After a child takes that new learning to independence, we teach to push the child into new learning. A child's zone of proximal development is always evolving.

The only way to know what a student knows and what he or she needs to know next to become a more proficient writer is to know the student. This takes time. Time spent sitting by the child watching the child write, talking with the child, and listening to the child. Students often give great answers to the question, "What do you think you need to know next to become a better writer?" We talk about it with them and decide together what to teach. Students will ask us to teach periods and how to "make people cry like Patricia Polacca does" or "make people laugh like Audrey and Don Wood do." The students are referring to mini-lessons or units we have taught in the past. Keeping a conversation on learning about writing going enables us to find out what our learners need to know next.

From whatever methods we have used to write down our ongoing assessments, we analyze them to drive our instruction for each child. We teach from our assessments, and then we hold the child accountable. If we are writing with a child and notice that there are no periods or that the word *they* is written *thay*, we let the child know we expect him or her to apply what has been learned. It is easy to look at our grid or card and say, "Sophay, you know how to put in periods. Read it again and put them in. I'll be right back to talk with you when it is easier for us to read." Or "Anh, go back and fix the spelling of *they* before you tape that poster up."

Writing is a process that takes time for children to learn. ELLs need to learn labeling language for their stories. They also need to learn academic vocabulary: *topic, draft, revise, edit, publish, comment, question, suggestion.* They need to learn social language: "Help me." "I like your illustration." They need to learn English structure to form a sentence, and they need to find their voice as writers. There are so many conventions and skills for children to learn. We know that it all can't be learned in a day, a month, or even a year. Children need the gift of time. They need time alone and with friends. They need time with an adult by their side. They will learn to write when given time, nurturing, and nudging.

5
READING WORKSHOP

I still choose books students will enjoy and weave our conversations around genres and author studies, but I am more deliberate now. I've learned to choose texts that will support the conversations we're having and offer experiences that will help students connect the stories we read to their lives, to other stories we have read together, or to the ways we make sense of our reading. I now choose books to support my teaching.

Cathy Mere, *More Than Guided Reading*

In Christine Sganga's first-grade classroom, Christine is rereading *Amber on the Mountain* by Tony Johnston to her class after lunch one day in October. Amber is a lonely girl living on a mountainside. A man arrives to build a road and his daughter Anna befriends Amber, teaching her to read. She has chosen this rereading as an illustration for her focus lesson on "rereading when you come to a tricky place." Several of the children are getting tired, and the wiggles are setting in. It is the second time they have heard the story, and Christine is reading it in its entirety, encouraging the children to interject comments. "There's flowers." "Is that where they milk the cow?" "Yuck! Eeugh!"

There is a lot to understand in this story. Ulises is banging his boot. Sharday asks José to move away from her because his fidgeting is bothering her. José goes off to the side of the group and sulks. He puts his face into a box of books and then starts looking at one.

Christine uses the signal she has practiced to refocus the class. She covers her eyes and counts to three. The children squiggle back to sitting positions, eyes on the book and hands in laps. They know the routine.

Ulises says, "They're reading a book and we're reading a book." Christine marks that page with a sticky note, saying, "Amber had to go back and start again when she was reading, didn't she?" José scoots closer and is back engaged with the text. Christine mouths, "Thank you for joining us" without missing a beat.

Later she says, "We're going to look at that page I marked again. Look. Amber did something very important that readers do here. Who knows what it was?" Zindy says, "She read it again." "Yes," replies Christine. "Readers go back and read again when they get to a tricky part. Watch me." Christine picks up a student's reading book and models how to reread at the point of difficulty. "When you go to your quiet spot with your book box, do you think you can try going back to reread when you get to a tricky part? Give me a thumbs up if you're going to practice rereading when you get to a tricky part." Thumbs shoot up. Christine dismisses one group at a time to go and get their book boxes and move to quiet spots around the room. As she walks around the room listening in on readers, Christine praises any rereading she hears.

Reading Workshop Structure Supports ELLs

In the example above, Christine had embedded her mini-lesson within a familiar read-aloud since the story leant itself to this. There are many different purposes that guide our book selection for the workshop introduction. We often begin reading workshop with a story that we want the students to enjoy. Listening for pleasure is an important skill. Sometimes it will be a second or third reading of a story that will build familiarity with the story, the language, or the content. This read-aloud, in turn, might be in preparation for a mini-lesson that is planned for the next day or the near future. We know that every time our ELLs hear a story, they are coming to a deeper understanding as they make connections to their own experiences and to other books. They are gaining knowledge of storybook language and learning new vocabulary.

After the story we teach a short mini-lesson. The focus of the lesson might require a story that engages the children in questioning and reflecting as we read. Or it might require a poem or the shared reading of a Big Book. The lesson will feature a teaching point selected because of student need and/or our Language Arts curriculum. We might focus on a comprehension strategy, a reading strategy, features of text or genre, or word work, to mention but a few. We follow the teaching with some time to discuss the teaching point, either in the whole group, in small groups, or with partners.

This discussion provides the opportunity for our ELLs to build understanding, practice vocabulary, and rehearse language structures with their peers in a nonthreatening situation. Our role is to check for understanding, clear up confusion, model structures, and teach vocabulary, adjusting our teaching based on the level of English acquisition of each student.

Discussion time is followed by small-group work or independent reading time. At the end of the reading workshop we call the children back together to review the teaching point and reflect on some of the good reading behaviors that we have observed during their independent work time.

In *Reading Essentials*, Regie Routman refers to the components of reading workshop as "demonstration, shared demonstration, guided practice, and independent practice" (2003). These stages of the workshop offer native speakers and English language learners alike the opportunity to take on a skill with just the right degree of support from teacher and peers.

Scaffolding Instruction During Shared Reading

Shared reading experiences can provide our ELLs with an introduction to the idea that readers always read for meaning. It is our thinking aloud and our modeling that helps them see that we read to understand. In kindergarten and first grade, much of the work to build a core of letter, word, and text knowledge occurs during shared literacy activities with the whole group. Our ELLs need to be actively participating in all these activities at whatever level is appropriate for their degree of language acquisition. We read together to discover the meaning of the text. It might be text that we have constructed together, such as our morning message or the shared writing of a class story; it might be our charts of poems and songs or our Big Books. Using this large clear print, we are able to address:

- Bringing meaning to text;
- Letter ID;
- Directionality in text;
- Visual features of letters and letter clusters;
- Sound-symbol relationships of letters and letter clusters;
- High-frequency words;
- Visual features of words;
- Visual patterns in words and text;
- Punctuation;
- Vocabulary;
- Reading with expression;
- Reading dialog;
- Reading with phrasing and fluency;
- Rehearsing language structures;
- Authors' craft; and more.

Since every child is at a different place in gaining control over each of these skills, the teacher must be sensitive to the degree of support needed to accommodate each learner.

Tess was recently reading the Big Book *Hattie and the Fox* (Mem Fox) to Leisha Lawrence's first graders. Jeyson had only recently arrived from El Salvador. He was in the preproductive stage of English acquisition. He was willing to point, nod, and say yes or no. Jeyson recognized the animals as the pictures drew him into the story. As Tess read the story, she was careful to point clearly to each animal as she said its name. Jeyson smiled and nodded.

Yaritza, also from El Salvador, had come to Bailey's at the beginning of first grade. She knew some of the animal names, and she was cheerfully chanting in all the right places. Alberto's family is from Cuba. He was fast approaching a stage of intermediate fluency, and he enjoyed getting his mouth around funny new phrases like "Goodness, gracious me!" Thanh, whose family is from Vietnam, was reading along fluently with several of the English speakers in the class.

Each of these students needed a different degree of support. As she read, Tess was constantly moving up and down the scale of support. She asked Jeyson to point to the animals as she named them in the story so that he could still be an active participant without responding orally. She leaned over to chime in with Yaritza as she chanted the phrases she knew. Tess interrupted the story briefly so everyone could rehearse, "Goodness, gracious me!" She did not want Alberto to feel he was the only one having difficulty with this phrase. As the children become more experienced in the literacy activities that we introduce them to during shared reading times, they are developing the skills they need in order to work independently.

Developing Independence with ELLs

How do you get reading workshop to run smoothly when you have students who speak little or no English, who don't know the names of the letters, or who have no idea about the sounds related to the letters? In a workshop setting, it is essential for students to be able to work independently so that the teacher is free to work one-on-one with students or with small groups.

Within the first week of school, we begin introducing the procedures for transitioning some of our whole-group literacy activities into independent reading activities so that individualized reading instruction can begin. We model activities clearly so that our ELLs know what is expected during each activity, during transitions, and during cleanup. These clear and consistent expectations are especially important to provide a degree of predictability throughout the day for the second language learners. They are confronted with so much that is new that any standard routine must offer a degree of security.

Independent Reading Time

After the whole-group read-aloud and mini-lesson, it is time to break up for independent reading. At this time, the students read from their own reading boxes. The boxes contain familiar books that they reread for practice. Each time they reread a book, their understanding deepens and their control of phrasing, fluency, and expression increases, so this is an essential element of our reading time. Their reading boxes also contain books that are at their instructional level, requiring them to do some reading work that is appropriate for them. (See Figure 5.1.) We have introduced all these books during guided reading lessons. Even the students who are preemergent readers have their own reading work to do independently. If they do not have appropriate-leveled text to hold their attention, they will become bored, reluctant to engage with the text, and possibly resort to distracting behavior.

A favorite lesson for some primary teachers at Bailey's to introduce children to the expectations of independent reading is a reading response to a Big Book called *Bubble Gum* by Gail Jorgensen. The children in the book learn to blow a bubble bigger and bigger and bigger. The last page has a great illustration of a popped bubble all over the children. The class enjoys acting

Figure 5.1 Kindergarteners Nahya and Jessica are engrossed in independent reading from their book boxes.

out an innovation on the text of *Bubble Gum*. Without speaking, they pretend to unwrap gum, stick it in their mouth, and blow and blow. As they blow, they spread their arms out wider and wider. They carefully walk with their arms spread out to a place in the room where no one can pop their bubble. If a child steps into or sits too close to someone's "bubble space" then the balloon pops. Loud words can also pop a bubble.

After the children can do this without fuss, the teacher explains that they will now take books inside their bubble to read alone. Later, after children learn to read independently in a bubble space, we show them how to let a friend come in and sit shoulder to shoulder in their bubble for buddy reading.

Buddy Reading

At the beginning of the year, teachers might find that there is a natural flow into this time of joyful book sharing and choose to establish the routines of buddy reading before those of independent reading. Buddy reading is an important option for reading work when students are not able to sustain independent reading for more than a short time. Buddy reading is important for many reasons.

Figure 5.2 Language is not a barrier when Thomas and Jonathan pair up for buddy reading.

- It is fun!
- Book discussions between students provide another opportunity for language development.
- It allows students alternative ways to engage with a variety of levels of text in a peer-coaching situation. For instance, ELLs can look at pictures and join in conversations about content even if they cannot read it themselves. (See Figure 5.2.)
- ELLs can talk in their home language to reach a deeper understanding of the book from the pictures.
- ELLs can practice reading books in pairs.
- Advanced readers can support each other in challenging text or content.

In order to establish a calm working atmosphere for buddy reading time, Tess clearly models her expectations in a "fishbowl." She demonstrates the procedure with one child as the others watch from the circle. She asks the students to comment on what they notice. They watch as Tess and her buddy discuss their choice of books at the bookshelf and then sit side by side with the books they have chosen, deciding which one to look at first. As Tess and her buddy talk quietly about the pictures or as one of them reads to the other, the students listen and hear them decide that they are ready to change books and then discuss what their next choices should be. Because the students have noticed all this, Tess knows that they are ready to practice this procedure themselves.

Then Tess joins the circle and asks two other students to model the procedure, again inviting brief comments from the class. She wants to move on quickly so that the whole class can practice the procedure. Tess names the ELLs, one by one, and tells them to pick a partner. She wants this first experience to be with a child with whom they feel comfortable interacting. Then Tess moves around the room, gently refocusing students on the expectations if necessary. After about ten minutes, the class meets back in the circle to reflect on how the experience went and discuss any modifications that might be necessary.

When it is time to practice this routine again the next day, the class helps to create a list of expectations first. For example:

1. Choose two books.
2. Sit side by side.
3. Sit at the same level.
4. Listen to the speaker.

It is simple to add pictures to this list so that the expectations are just as clear to the second language learners. The list is a reminder that can be revisited at any time.

The fishbowl technique can provide invaluable guided practice in many situations. It clarifies expectations for all students, but it is also a helpful way of making sure our ELLs see and experience the expectations with the group. There is then less chance of them misunderstanding directions, doing something the wrong way, or embarrassing themselves in front of their peers.

Our buddy reading expectations usually begin with pairs of children going to the library corner and choosing two books each. We talk about suitable spots for reading and places to avoid (like behind the door), and then the children are free to take their books anywhere in the room within the teacher's sight to read, to look at illustrations, and to talk. Therefore, you will find children under the tables, squeezed into nooks and crannies, or sitting on our feet under the reading table as we work with other students (a great spot for ELLs to be absorbing reading behaviors!).

There are many ways to structure this time that depend on teaching style, schedules, class size, and makeup. But for us, the nonnegotiables are the elements of book choice and the opportunity for talk. Thus, we might modify our framework to involve more or less structure, depending on the needs of each year's class. We might ask them to read the books in their book boxes to each other, or let them choose to do this if they wish. If necessary, we will pair up our ELLs with students who will be good language or behavior role models.

Sometimes we want to designate the partners for a particular learning or social purpose, but more often than not, we want the ELLs to have an opportunity to enjoy books with a friend, perhaps being able to talk in their home language about the text. Having an opportunity to discuss concepts or content in their home language is going to give the ELLs a chance to expand their understandings. These understandings provide the knowledge around which they can begin to build their English vocabulary and control of sentence structure.

Establishing Expectations for Reading Workshop

During independent reading and buddy reading time, we are free to pull aside our guided reading groups. We base the groupings on the children's reading needs and remain flexible throughout the year as their needs change. Sometimes we work with small groups, and sometimes it is necessary to provide one-on-one instruction. Once all the children are reading from book boxes, or buddy reading, we ask a group to quietly break away from their reading task to come and read with us for a while and then return to their task.

We need to manage this reading time efficiently so that we are able to hear as many readers as possible. It is essential, therefore, that the routines and expectations of reading workshop are in place and we know the students can work independently.

Grouping Students for Reading Instruction

Next, we need to consider how to group our students, giving careful thought to the needs of our ELLs. Along with literacy skills, we must bear in mind their control of English, social skills, self-esteem, and attention span when sharing the teacher's attention with others. We ponder whether we can best meet their needs in a group, paired, or individually.

To set up her reading schedule in first grade, Tess looks at the blocks of time that are available for small-group instruction and decides how many groups or individuals she can expect to work with during those times. She then looks at her class list and groups the students with similar needs together. She tries to keep the groups to four students or less for two reasons. A larger group might mean that it is difficult to meet the needs of the ELLs with a variety of language experience and keep them all on task during a

97

book introduction. And, sometimes, it is just hard to find more than four copies of a particular book to introduce to students.

Tess sets up her schedule so that she will meet more frequently with the students who need the most support. Many of the second language learners are going to fall into this category. She tries to work with these groups four times a week. She will work with stronger readers who need less support three times a week and meet twice a week with her strongest readers.

Sometimes we decide to read with students individually, particularly early on in the year, because ELLs need our full attention. A newcomer in any grade may also need individual attention for a while before joining a group. As we see that the students are ready to focus and participate with others, we will work with groups of two or three.

Reading Instruction for ELLs

What's in a Name?

For many children entering kindergarten, both English speakers and English learners, one of the first challenges is learning to read their own name. They have to recognize which grouping of black squiggles represents their name; therefore, we begin the year with many name activities. (See Figure 5.3.) We are able to teach letters and sounds within the context of each child's name right from the beginning of the year. We continue to focus on phonemic awareness and phonetic work with ever-expanding text.

Tess spreads out the name tags on the table closest to the door. The children place their names in a basket as they arrive in the morning. Later, a student is responsible for reporting the names of any absent students to the class. Emelie asks her students to sign in as they arrive. This establishes a reading/writing connection from the beginning. Even though some of the kindergarteners are not yet capable of writing their names clearly, Emelie is honoring their attempts, knowing that they will improve.

Other teachers have a pocket for each child on a chart outside the door and ask the children to turn their name cards over as they arrive.

Children begin the year reading names. We post names for class jobs, insert them into songs and poems on the pocket chart, include them in shared writing, and place them clearly on student work. We label coat hooks, book boxes, work mats, and more. Names provide a starting point for many early reading activities that we introduce to the whole class or use for whole-group practice and small-group reinforcement or independent work at choice time.

Carolina joined Tess's first-grade class in February. She had come from El Salvador and had never been to school before. The reading workshop rou-

Figure 5.3 Mary makes her name with magnetic letters.

tine was running smoothly, and Tess needed to welcome Carolina into the routine without disrupting the other students' reading instruction for too long. But she could not just let Carolina sit.

After spending some time with Carolina, Tess assigned Maria to be her mentor since she spoke English quite well and was a mother hen by nature. One of the earliest activities Carolina could work on independently was to match names to laminated photos of her classmates. She began with her own name and picture and moved on to Maria's. With Maria's help, she quickly added more names those first few days. Using the name cards and photos, Tess made up greeting activities for the class morning meeting.

Maria helped Carolina find the appropriate magnetic letters to match some of the names. Carolina could then take the cookie sheet containing the letters to use as her reading work. The whole class enjoyed revisiting some of the rhymes and songs in which they switched names on the charts. They added a "Carolina" page to our *Mary Wore Her Red Dress* class book: "Carolina wore her blue jeans."

The following are interactive name activities to engage ELLs:

- Substitute children's names in songs and poems. (Hector jumped over the candle stick.)
- Create class books based on favorite stories. (José went walking, what did he see?)
- Build names with magnetic letters or letter cards in a pocket chart.
- Include children's names with their photos on the word wall.
- Match photos of children with their names.
- Use names on magnetic cards to graph answers to questions such as Do you like pizza? Yes or No.

Individualized Alphabet Rings

Many of our newcomers do not know the alphabet in their own language or in English, so learning to recognize and name the letters is one of the first academic challenges many of our students face.

Carolina needed initial success in learning a few letters really well. The purpose was to give her the experience of *how* to learn letters so that she could apply this knowledge as she continued to learn more letters. Fortunately, Carolina's name consists of letters that are visually distinctive and that were useful in helping her link her letter knowledge to other words (*can*, *run*, *play*, *on*, and so on).

In order to start teaching Carolina the letter names, Tess wrote *Carolina* on an index card. C was the first letter Carolina needed to learn. The other consonants, *r*, *l*, and *n*, were the dominant sounds in her name and would be useful letters for Carolina to learn next. Tess wrote each letter on an index card and put them on a binder ring. Carolina kept this ring of letters in her book box, and Tess added letters as the girl learned them. O was next, as it is a distinctively easy shape for children to learn. Tess practiced these letters with Carolina each day, and so did Maria. Maria decided Carolina should have a ring of letters for Maria's name too, so they made this together and added it to Carolina's book box.

During the early days, Carolina's reading work included making the letters with clay, writing them with colored glue, painting them, and so on. A tray of magnetic letters was on hand for identifying, matching, and sorting.

Individualized Alphabet Books

Once a child knows approximately ten alphabet letters, we make a personal alphabet book for that child. In preparation for this, we ask volunteers to put together blank books made of card stock at the beginning of the year. Each book has thirteen pages so that the children can start working with the rules of directionality, turning the pages, reading the left page first, and reading from left to right across each page. Going from left to right, each page shows only the upper-case letter, the lower-case letter, and a picture (but no label) of an object that the child knows by name. This object is the child's choice—a personal link in order to remember this letter and its sound more easily. The teacher can use this picture hook to support the child as he or she learns to connect the sound of the letter to what is seen (the sound-symbol connection). These sound-symbol connections will be essential as the student begins to read and write.

Once Carolina recognized about ten letters, Tess began an alphabet book for her. She included only the letters Carolina knew, counting each upper-case and lower-case letter as separate letters. The first few pages of Carolina's alphabet book read like this: A, *a, apple* B, *b, banana*, C, *c, cat*, D, *dog* (she did not know lower-case *d*) blank page (she did not know E or *e*), *f, fish*, and so on. The decision to begin with only known letters was deliberate. Tess did not want to confuse Carolina with letters that she could not yet identify. She wanted her to build confidence working with the familiar.

During shared reading and writing workshop, Tess would introduce new letters and links to Carolina. As Carolina learned more letters or picture hooks, Tess added them to her alphabet book. She was then able to refer to this book to help Carolina make connections. "You know a word that starts like this. It starts like *fish* in your alphabet book. How will you start to say this word?" Or, "How would you write *friend*? It starts with the same sound as *fish*. Let's look in your alphabet book."

Tess did not want to limit Carolina's access to books just because the girl did not know all the letters, so in Carolina's book box Tess included a C book, an N book, and so on. She put in alphabet books and nonfiction books with interesting illustrations that Carolina could enjoy as well as some teacher-made books and one or two of the clearly illustrated texts used for read-aloud. This way, Carolina had plenty of text to look at when it was independent reading time and to share with friends at buddy reading time. Carolina needed to engage with familiar pictures and stories, even though they were beyond her reading ability at this point. (See Figure 5.4.)

Teaching for Early Reading Behaviors

During our Language Arts blocks at the beginning of the year, so much shared reading and writing occurs. We model early reading behaviors and "think aloud" to the children so that they start to become aware of the rules of print. We cannot assume that they come with an understanding of these early behaviors. We need to teach them explicitly to children, like many of our newcomers, who have had very limited experience with text.

Figure 5.4 The contents of Carolina's book box soon after she arrived mid-year.

In *Becoming Literate*, Dr. Marie Clay states, "Teachers cannot assume that beginning readers can isolate for attention the things the labels refer to. If they cannot and the teacher uses the terms without checking the teaching-learning interaction goes astray." Clay goes on to say, "If the teacher examines the things she says to her class, to small groups, and to individual children she may find that she takes for granted insights which some children do not have" (1991). For example, we have learned that we cannot assume a child knows the difference between a letter and a word.

Early Reading Behaviors

Through exposure at home and in the classroom children develop an awareness of the earliest behaviors needed to reach the meaning of text. Certain behaviors need to be mastered in order for the child to focus on the appropriate print.

- One-to-one matching
- Control of directionality
- Monitoring for known words
- Monitoring for unknown words

One-to-one Matching

This is an initial stage in coming to understand the connection between oral language and our written code. The reader has to understand that each group of black squiggles represents one word and that each word brings us closer to divining the meaning carried in the text. At this early stage, we need the children to point under each word as they read in order to internalize the link between voice and print. Once they control this skill, they will no longer need to point. The ability to point accurately is going to give the children an early way to monitor their accuracy in reading. We can teach them that if they get to the end of a line of print and their finger is not under the last word, something is wrong and they need to try it again.

In order to develop this one-to-one matching, we begin with pictures of labeled objects. We use little books that have a picture on one page and the word on the next page. We use simple picture dictionaries. We use books that label a picture with the article and the name, for example, "the milk, the eggs" or "a ball, a bat, a bee." The goal is to get the child to point to the word and associate the spoken word with the group of black squiggles on the page.

As the child gains control of this matching, we need to move towards working with texts that have simple sentences of three or four words on one single line. Since we do not talk in labels—"the ball, the cat, the boy"—we soon need to expose our ELLs to more natural structures that they are going to hear in English. Thus, we can quickly expand labels to a short sentence structure. "The ball is here. The cat is here. The boy is here." "I like the cat. I like the baby."

We never seem to have enough leveled books in the classroom for all our emergent readers, so we supplement with teacher-made books if necessary. This allows us to construct the text specifically for each student, which is important for our ELLs. Carolina did not know about farms or zoos when she first arrived in this country, but she did know about shopping with her mom at the store. After a brief chat about going to the store, Tess was able to make a little book that read: "I see the apple. I see the banana. I see the milk. I see the eggs." Tess already had little blank books stapled together, so she could quickly write a single line of text on each page and put the correct sticker on that page as a reminder of the word.

Since Tess did not want Carolina to think that reading was being able to remember label words, that is, vocabulary, she also included text like "Carolina is here. Carolina is not here." And, using pictures of classmates, "I see Carolina. I see Maria. I see Elliot."

Possible materials to have on hand in the classroom for book making include:

- Teacher-made blank books for ABC books (thirteen pages) and for text (six to eight pages)
- Stickers: animals, food, and so on
- *Bookbuilder* software
- Index cards and binder rings
- Multiple copies of each child's photo

We type or write simple pattern sentences on a single line and use stickers as illustrations to scaffold meaning for the reader. The text might read, "I see a dog. I see a cat," and so on. Since a child will quickly memorize such patterned structures, this type of text is only useful for gaining control of voice-print match and the early monitoring behaviors of identifying known and unknown words. Real reading work will take place in less predictable text later.

Tess could introduce a teacher-made text in this way: "Carolina, this book is all about things you can see. Let's take a look at the pictures. What's this? Yes, it's a cat. What can you see here? Oh, look. Here's a dog. That's right. You can see a dog. Now I want you to read this book with your finger, Carolina." As Carolina reads, Tess might say, "Carolina, you made your finger match the words. Well done!" or, "Uh, oh! There weren't enough words were there? Try that again."

If Carolina appears confused, or struggles to match her voice to the text, Tess can jump in and say, "Let me help you match your finger to the words." Or, as Carolina turns the page, "Remember this is the page about the rabbit," giving her the unfamiliar vocabulary. Thus, Tess is prepared to move up and down that scale of support, gauging how much Carolina needs based on her responses. Tess does not want her to become confused or to think that reading is hard.

Like any one of us, Carolina is going to enjoy things that she does well, giving her the confidence to take more risks and be an active participant in the work of reading. If she thinks she cannot do it, she is not going to try, but will wait passively until the teacher jumps in and does the work for her and her progress will be minimal. We must guarantee opportunities for our ELLs to experience success.

Control of Directionality

Children need to understand that the rules applying to directionality never vary. In English, we always go from left to right and then we sweep back to the left of the next line, moving from top to bottom down the page. Once Carolina mastered voice-print match, Tess was able to introduce two lines of text on a page, so that the girl could practice matching her voice to the print when she had to move her finger back to the beginning of the next line. Tess created text like, "I like to play   with my ball."

Teachers need to be alert to those children who might be demonstrating confusion over these rules, so that they can model correctly and explicitly during shared reading of large print in Big Books and on charts and during guided reading. Our ELLs might have experience with a written code that has different rules of directionality. They might just be trying to construct their own rules based on misunderstandings and think it is of no consequence if you track left to right or right to left or do a mix of both. We cannot afford to assume that they understand. Therefore, we must be explicit in our language as we model: "I'm going to start reading right here. I always go this way, and now I have to come back down over here, and go this way again."

Monitoring for Known Words

Soon Carolina was able to recognize a few words. She was able to recognize *Carolina, mom, I, the,* and *a* in a variety of different places (on charts, in the morning message, in books). She was also able to write these anchor words, and they made up her reading and writing vocabulary in these early days. She could check to see if her finger was under the word *mom* as she said it. If the text read, "I see mom," Carolina would know that she was correct as she read and pointed to *I* and *mom*.

Locating these words as she read enabled her to monitor herself to know whether she was in the right place or not. If her finger was bouncing along slower than her voice was reading, and she read *mom* when her finger was under *see*, she might look up at Tess, knowing something was wrong. The simple teacher prompt, "Try that again," would help her develop the strategy to go back and reread.

To allow Carolina to confirm what words she knows, Tess might ask her to find *mom* or *is* on a page during the book introduction. After Carolina reads, Tess might reinforce reading the words correctly by saying, "When your finger was under this word you said 'mom.' You were really checking that that was the word *mom*, weren't you? Well done!" This specific praise reinforces the behavior of checking.

Monitoring for Unknown Words

Carolina also needed to learn that she could monitor her reading using unknown words. (Later she will learn how to solve unknown words. For now, she is still at the very early stages of reading.) If Carolina kept reading predictable text, she might conclude that reading is just guessing what the words are based on the pattern. To prevent this, Tess needed easy text that included Carolina's known words but that was not constructed in a predictable pattern, so once again, she needed to make her own books. These were simply a few sheets of copy paper folded and stapled.

Using a combination of known and predictable unknown words, and illustrating with an animal sticker on each page for support, Tess created text such as the following:

> Carolina said, "Here is the cat."
> Mom said, "Here is the dog."
> "Here is the bird," said Mom.
> "The fish is here," said Carolina.

This text uses Carolina's known words—*Carolina, mom, the*—as anchors to enable her to monitor herself. The unknown word *said* and the names of the animals remain predictable; Carolina expects the animal words to be there even though they are not among her known words. Because the order of the words does not conform to a stable pattern, Carolina has to monitor herself and confirm her own reading, rather than just rattling off a repetitive structure. This book forces Carolina to pay attention to print and recognize the words she knows and predict the ones she does not know.

In *Becoming Literate*, Dr. Marie Clay says that "the beginning reader has to give attention to visual information as well as the language and messages but gradually becomes able to use visual information without much conscious attention, freeing more attention for the messages and language of the text and for novel information which expands the system" (1991). Thus, the teacher's conversation during the book introduction might go as follows:

"Here is a book about some animals you and your mom see. You tell me what animals mom and Carolina see, and I'll tell you what they say."

Next, Tess wants Carolina to confirm some of her known words. "Show me *Carolina* [known]. Good. Show me *the* [known]. Uh-huh. Now show me *cat* [unknown]. That's right. You had two ways to check it. This part is about the cat, isn't it? So that makes sense. And *cat* starts like *Carolina*, doesn't it?

"Yes. You remembered Mom was going to say 'Here is the dog,' didn't you? Show me *here* [unknown].

"Let's read the first page together. Now you try this page."

Tess remained ready to jump in with more support and do a shared reading of the whole book the first time through, if necessary. She wanted to keep the reading work easy.

Another support for making simple text is the *Bookbuilder* CD published by Literacy Footprints. Using this software, Tess was able to insert Carolina's name in preprinted text with simple, engaging illustrations. Taking into account Carolina's bank of known words, it was possible to find text suitable for Carolina, given her experiences and word recognition.

Book Selection for Guided Reading

We cannot wait until our ELLs have enough language to use structures we commonly encounter in text, and we do not wait for them to learn some of the unfamiliar vocabulary they will come across. In order for these students to have the same opportunity as every other child to experience success as a reader right from the start, they need to be reading books just like everyone else in the class. We believe children learn to read by reading. Therefore, we expect to give them a high degree of support as we introduce them to new language structures and vocabulary. We consider both as we search for books to introduce to our ELLs.

Book selection is important. We avoid books using nonsense language or contrived rhyming structures or books that are difficult to predict. We pass over books about topics with which our ELLs have no experience, such as snow skiing. We look for a story line that will be predictable, based on children's own experiences, although we do not expect them to know all the vocabulary. We just accept that there will be new words that we will have to help them with.

The text we select needs to contain a good number of the students' known words, which they can use as anchors. If there are words that seem to be ongoing problems—for instance, confusing *can* with *come*—we will select text that contains only one of these words often, so we can practice it and clear up the confusion. We consider language structures that we find in the text but are not in the English language learner's oral language patterns—for example, "Late last night" or "Home we go"—that will need to be rehearsed before reading the text. Finding text that is just right for each second language learner is not an easy feat!

Book Introductions

We set our students up for success through the way in which we introduce a book to them. We need to consider what to point out during this brief conversation and rehearsal time. First, we set the scene by giving a short summary in which we try to make a connection to children's experiences or to other books they might have read. "This book is about picking apples. Do you remember when you went to the apple orchard in kindergarten?" Or, "This book is about picking apples. Look, here's Kira again. Do you remember the story about Dad making pancakes for breakfast? Kira was in that story too."

In the book *Emily's Babysitter* by Michelle Dufresne, Emily is left with a babysitter, who tries to play with her, but Emily refuses to join in. However, when the babysitter finally offers to read a story, Emily responds happily. Here is a possible way to introduce the book.

"This story is about a little girl whose mom and dad leave her with a babysitter. Have you ever had to stay with a babysitter when your mom and dad go somewhere? Well, Emily does not want to play with the babysitter. But, at the end of the story, the babysitter finds something that Emily likes to do. Let's take a look. You can guess who this is, can't you?

"You know *Here* and *is*. Which word is *babysitter*? You're right. How did you know? Right, it starts with 'buh' like *ball*, and it's a big word isn't it?

"Oh, what do you think Emily called to her mom and dad here?" (We know that *called* is a new word for the child, so we feed it into the conversation.)

Consider the structure of these two sentences: "'Emily, look,' said the babysitter. 'We can swim in the pool.'" This might be tricky for an ELL to read fluently. We might need to say, "Let's practice this. Listen. Now say it with me. Good. Now you try it. Good. You really sounded like the babysitter talking. Now you read *Emily's Babysitter* and think about what Emily and the babysitter say." After the student has read the book to us, we tuck the book away in our file, ready to do a running record as the child reads the text the next day.

Assessment

Running records are a powerful reading assessment tool. A running record is a way of accurately recording a student's reading of a text and allows teachers to determine whether a text is at the student's instructional level. This means the text will allow the student to work in his or her zone of proximal development. There is some reading work to be done that will stretch the child, but it is not so difficult that the child will become confused, or so easy that no learning will take place.

All attempts and errors are recorded, enabling the teacher to track patterns of responses and the types of errors made. With this information, the teacher can plan the reading instruction in order to teach explicitly to introduce new learning or to correct errors, misunderstandings, or confusion.

This powerful tool for guiding reading instruction is used across the grade levels. Each year our reading teachers provide training for new teachers who are unfamiliar with this form of assessment. The teachers learn to take running records and analyze them to see which strategies students attend to and which ones they neglect, in order to know what to teach next. For further reading on this form of assessment, see *Running Records: a Self-Tutoring Guide* by Peter H. Johnston.

We record the date, title of book introduced, new vocabulary, and any problems the child encounters during the initial reading in each child's record folder. The next day, we listen to the child read the new text in order to take the running record. After taking the running record, we select one teaching point to work on immediately in the text.

If the book is at the child's instructional level—that is, read with 90 percent accuracy or above—we put it into the child's book box and it becomes a familiar text to reread at independent reading time or with a friend at buddy reading time. If the book proves slightly challenging, we might read it together a few times before putting it in the book box.

We examine the running records to see what kinds of errors readers are making. We can then explicitly teach strategies to help the children avoid these errors. So if ELLs are attending to visual information only (that is, graphophonic cues) we can teach them how to think about the meaning of the story and try a word that would make sense, given that the word begins with a certain letter or cluster of letters.

Integrating Information from Different Sources During Text Reading

In order to read fluently, children need to process information from different sources with automaticity. Readers have to take into account and integrate three major sources of information in text to come up with one correct solution. The word has to make sense in the story (meaning); it has to be structurally correct (syntax); it has to look right (graphophonic information). Readers are able to move forward in thinking about the story and the anticipated language structure without being locked into a word-by-word approach.

The Importance of Reading with Fluency for ELLs

One aspect of reading that is important to focus on with ELLs is the ability to sound phrased and fluent. Second language learners will not necessarily pick up the natural phrasing of the language by listening to spoken English. If they read word by word, they will sound monotone and lifeless. When they do this, each word presents itself as a problem to be solved in isolation from the context of the words around it. Reading in a phrased and fluent way allows the reader to predict what is coming next and maintain the meaning of the story and the flow of the language. Therefore, we need to make sure that we attune ELLs to fluent reading during our read-alouds.

However, we also need to teach explicitly for fluency, rehearsing how words are grouped together during our book introductions. Many second language learners do not instinctively know which words are grouped together in story reading, so they might read "said the babysitter" word by word, resulting in a choppy sound, rather than as a smoothly fluent phrase.

Let's consider introducing Michele Dufresne's book *Picking Apples* to a second language learner who is reading word by word in a robotic way, with little or no intonation. The teacher has deliberately picked a book that will be easy for this child to read. The story line is straightforward, and the child knows most of the words. The child must be free to attend to the way the reading sounds instead of working on reading the words.

The first page reads:

"Come on," said Mom.
"We are going to go
and pick apples. Then we
can make apple pie
and apple sauce."

Teacher: Look at those girls! They look very excited about going to pick apples, don't they? Can you see Mom has the car keys in her hand? What do you think Mom might be saying to Kira?

Child: "Come on, girls"?

Teacher: You're right! She is saying, "Come on." Now, how does your mom sound when she says, "Come on"?

Child: "COME ON!"

Teacher: Good. Now let's make Kira's mom say it like that. You try it.

Child: Come on!

Teacher: Wow! You really sounded like a mom then. Now I'm going to put my fingers here to show you which words go together in groups. [The teacher frames "Come on" with her index finger and thumb from above the words. Then she does the same with "said Mom."] I want you to read the words you can see together like this. [The teacher reads "Come on" and then "said Mom" with a momentary pause between the phrases.] Now you try it.

Child: [Reads first line with expression as two phrases.]

Teacher: Now let's do that with the rest of this page. [And she frames the phrases like this: We are going / to go / and pick apples. / Then / we can make / apple pie / and apple sauce. /]

Child: [Reads in phrases.]

Teacher: My goodness! Did you hear how you sounded? You sounded like a grown-up reader. Let's try that on the other pages. I'll show you which words go together, and you read them like that.

With the right support on easy text, and lots of praise, this child will begin to take on this phrasing independently. The teacher will help the child pick up the pace so the reading soon sounds fluent. This skill will help the child hold on to the meaning of a story as he or she moves into more challenging text. When readers can predict a phrase in a story, then they no longer have to solve every single word. Reading with fluency allows them to feel the flow of the story so that their minds are predicting what will come next and they can confirm their predictions by checking to see if the words look right.

Teaching Language Structures to ELLs

Teaching language structures is a little different than teaching for fluency, although they certainly go hand in hand. We have all had the experience of saying to a second language learner, "Did that sound right?" After a quick glance at our faces to try to read the answer we are expecting, the child nods. So often, ELLs do not have enough experience with language to know what sounds right and what does not. They have not been listening to and absorbing English structures since birth. Therefore, we must counteract this lack of experience with rehearsal of structures during our book introductions and text reading.

Here is another example from *Picking Apples:*

"Oh, this green apple
looks good, too,"
said Kira,
and she took a bite.

This is a complex sentence for second language learners to read fluently and could require some rehearsal. To provide support, we follow the procedure to gradually release responsibility to students. We begin by modeling and then share the task, asking students to do it with us. Next, we ask them to try it alone, while we are prepared to jump in with support, until they are able to take on the task independently.

Teacher: To make this sound good we have to read all the way to here [pointing to the comma after Kira] without stopping. It sounds like this, "'Oh, this green apple looks good, too,' said Kira." You try it.

Child: Oh, this green, this green apple, green apple looks . . .

Teacher: Listen again. [Repeats line.] Now you try it with me. [Child and teacher repeat line together.] Great job. Now try it again. [Child repeats line successfully.] That sounded good, but we didn't get it all yet. We have to read all the way to the period and make it sound really smooth. Listen to me. [Teacher reads page.] Let's try that together.

This guided rehearsal plants the sound of this sentence structure in the ear of the student. When reading the text a few moments later, the child will successfully read this complex sentence.

Self-Selection Baskets

Student choice is an important element of any workshop. Students choose their own writing topics, solve math problems in their own way, create their own science experiments. Our readers also need to choose their own appropriate books. This independence is important for all readers whatever their level of language or reading proficiency. As the year progresses and the children are all reading a wide range of texts, we want to add to the books we continue to select for them by giving them opportunities to choose their own.

One way to do this is to group books by levels in baskets, labeling each basket with the names of the children who may choose books from that basket. The books are ones that will be easy for everyone in that group to read. In *What Really Matters for Struggling Readers*, Richard L. Allington says that young readers need to read many books that are easy, so we try to have plenty of choices available. We model how the children may select a certain number of books from the basket, returning others, at buddy reading time.

We are convinced that children learn to read by reading, and so are the children. One day, Mary Anne Buckley had introduced a book to two of her kindergarteners, Jennry and Oscar. It was about bumper cars, and they had chatted first about riding on these. One of the boys knew what they were, and one didn't. Now they were sitting on either side of Mary Anne reading the book by themselves for the first time. As Mary Anne leaned over to work with Jennry, she heard a sharp gasp beside her. As she turned around, Oscar gasped again and, raising both hands triumphantly to the sky, joyfully proclaimed, "The words came down!" At that moment, everything he had been learning clicked into place, and he realized he was actually reading.

SOCIAL STUDIES WORKSHOP

Understanding must be earned. Whereas facts can be memorized and skills developed through drill and practice, coming to an understanding of "big ideas" requires students to construct meaning for themselves.

Carol Ann Tomlinson and Jay McTighe, *Integrating Differentiated Instruction and Understanding by Design*

At the end of January our student teacher, Lauren Nye, came back to visit us. She had left in October after six short weeks with us. Emelie casually asked the class to talk about what Ms. Nye had missed while she was gone. It was so exciting to hear what they still remembered as they recalled what they had learned.

"We was cooking corn."

"Long, long ago, they don't have food much. People sleep on hay on the floor."

"The Pilgrims died because they were so hungry and cold and they didn't wash their hands."

"Squanto help the Pilgrims to hunt deer and turkey."

"You can eat them."

"They cook them on a fire."

"They no have pockets in clothes."

"Or cars."

"No refrigerators."

"No TVs."

"They use candles."

"We make pockets like the Pilgrims."

"The children do chores. We do chores too."

"The Wampanoag make a long house and a canoe."

"They got guns. They shoot animals so they could eat."

This went on for quite awhile. The drama and movement activities of getting on the Mayflower, traveling across the ocean all scrunched up and sick, finding land, hunting for food, building homes, washing clothes, gardening, and doing all manner of chores had shown up in their dramatic play and their writing in November. Now at the end of January the vocabulary and understandings were still flowing out of the children.

District and state objectives drive our social studies curriculum (history, geography, economics, and civics). Our challenge is how to make such abstract concepts—the change rendered by the passage of time, long ago, distance, the relationship of self to the greater world—comprehensible to all young students. Our greater challenge is to ensure that our ELLs grasp our explanations. We realize the explanations and terms are layered with meaning, but we also know that the areas of focus are universal no matter what your language, culture, or country of origin. ELLs come to school with many experiences. Their experiences may be different from their peers' but those experiences can be used to make meaning of new content material. We must tap into these experiences and help them make connections.

Just imagine, as English language learners, sitting in a circle of students, gazing up expectantly at the teacher, and hearing, "A very long time ago people known as Pilgrims set sail across the ocean in search of a new home where they were free to worship as they pleased." Or "There are many ancient civilizations around the world that have made contributions to our lives today in America." What could these little learners possibly make of these statements?

To meet these challenges we plan units of study that progressively extend and build background knowledge. Through a cycle of exploration and discovery, observation, recording and reflection, we build on the students' understanding. Through visual images in nonfiction text and web sites, artifacts, acting, retelling, reading, writing, re-creating, art, and movement we attempt to make abstract concepts more real and comprehensible to the children.

Integrating Social Studies into Language Arts Workshops

We teach social studies during language arts. Our language arts curriculum includes storytelling; reading and writing for a purpose; nonfiction vs. fiction; using a table of contents, index, and glossary; and discerning important information, asking questions, and researching answers. We teach these language arts objectives while teaching the history, geography, economics, and civics curricula. Just as we often combine math and science lessons, we also combine social studies and language arts lessons.

The literature for read-aloud or mini-lessons during reading/writing workshop is often about the social studies topic. This gives children opportunities to use social studies vocabulary for extended periods in various settings.

We search library shelves for beautiful picture books that will give children background knowledge and help them understand the terms or concepts. For example, *Yonder* by Tony Johnston and *The Story of a Farm* by John S. Goodall are used to illustrate the passage of time and change over time. We find posters and magazines and search for web sites about our subject. Children learn to sort nonfiction and fiction books on the subject. They write nonfiction and other pieces. They write lists and diagrams and make posters. They label pictures and create Venn diagrams, T-charts, and lists of questions. These learning opportunities take place initially alongside an adult for guided practice and later on independently in small groups.

We integrate many other language arts skills and strategies into reading and writing during a social studies unit. Through such a unit of study, we teach the children to draw conclusions as they explore nonfiction text. They learn to analyze pictures and search for answers to questions. Children learn

115

how to put sticky notes on important pages and how to ask questions as they listen and read.

Exploring text becomes a practical strategy when students are designing period clothing, painting murals, making model houses, canoes, or fishing nets. Students rely on the text for information that will help them create their projects. They examine illustrations, photographs, and paintings as an effective way to glean information.

An effective way in which we guide children to a deeper understanding of a concept or content is through the use of a drama strategy called a tableau. A tableau is a living picture students create with their bodies. It is an effective learning tool for ELLs because a great deal of information can be delivered visually or kinesthetically as opposed to verbally. After an in-depth analysis of a word, a concept, or a unit of study, students arrange themselves into a living picture that interprets and shows understandings of important aspects of study. Creating a tableau of the image allows students to internalize and synthesize their understanding while bringing their own sense of expression to the process. They might create a picture of a Native American carrying a deer to reinforce the concept of hunters and gatherers. They might create a picture of people plowing a field to demonstrate that in early America families grew their own food, or they might depict George Washington crossing the Delaware River to interpret a visual image.

A class can create a series of tableaux that sequence an entire unit, chapter, or book. The tableau is motionless so the audience can look carefully at the scene. Slowly, each part of the tableau unfreezes, and the students say a word or line that describes or defines who their character is, what they are doing, or what they are thinking or feeling in that moment. They can then rearrange themselves to interpret a subsequent scene. Tableaux can be used successfully as both a learning experience and a performance to share student learning. (See Figure 6.1.)

Planning for Social Studies Units and Lessons

Grade-level teams work on social studies units about change over time, or as the children say, "long, long ago." We plan how to integrate the curriculum in the language arts block. As in all units of study, we plan to draw on the cultural diversity of our population. Our program of studies establishes our goals and objectives. We follow Backward Design planning from *Understanding by Design* by Grant Wiggins and Jay McTighe.

Figure 6.1 Jonathan sleeps at the foot of the Great Kapok tree (José) as the animals plead for the tree's survival.

We begin by deciding which essential understandings we want all students to come away with from the unit. As we teach, we find that there may be parts of the units we need to rethink. The children show us which parts we need to change for the next day or for the next year. The units are works in progress. Change over time and basic needs are universal to social studies curricula. The following is an example of a portion of a kindergarten unit of study using the Backward Design method of planning.

STAGE 1—DESIRED RESULTS

Established Goal(s) Basic Needs and Change Over Time

Social Studies Standards K1, 2, 6, 7
1. The student will recognize that history describes events and people of other times and places by identifying the people and events honored by the holiday of Thanksgiving Day.
2. The student will describe everyday life in the present and in the past and begin to recognize that things change over time.
3. The student will identify the difference between basic needs (food, clothing, and shelter) and wants (things people would like to have).
4. The student will recognize that people use money to purchase goods.

Social Studies Standard K.4
The student will use simple maps and globes to
1. Develop an awareness that a map is a drawing of a place to show where things are located and that a globe is a round model of the Earth;
2. Describe places referenced in stories and real-life situations;
3. Locate land and water features.

Visual Arts-ArtsEdge Standards
Content Standard 4—Understand the visual arts in relation to history and cultures.
Content Standard 1—Understand and apply media techniques and process (pottery and clay).

Theater
Content Standard 2—Act by assuming roles and interacting in improvisations.
Content Standard 3—Design by visualizing and arranging environments for classroom dramatizations.

Long Ago (Past/Present)

Understandings

Students will understand that . . .
- Every individual has basic needs, such as transportation, shelter, clothes, food, family, and survival.
- We learn from change over time.
- Certain people and events are associated with traditional holidays.
- Maps and globes are resources for locating places.
- People move for various reasons.
- Imagination can be used to role play characters from another time.
- Cooperation is a tool for learning.
- Voice is a tool for learning.
- Art is a tool for expressing what you see and feel.

Students will know . . .
- We express ourselves in storytelling, art, and drama.
- How to use their imagination, cooperation, and concentration when role playing characters from long ago.

Essential Questions

- How is the past about you?
- What is the difference between a want and a need?
- How do people today meet their basic needs? How did people in the past?
- What if you had lived long ago, how would your life be different? Why?
- How is life harder or easier now than long ago?
- Why do people create and use maps?
- What and how do we celebrate?
- How have celebrations changed over the years?
- What are you thinking when you are pretending long ago?
- What can we learn from studying the art of others?
- Why do people move?

Students will be able to . . .
- Separate fact from fiction. Use information from print and nonprint sources (pictures, music, traditional stories, family stories).

- The holidays we celebrate today are based on events that happened long ago.
- We honor the historical figures Squanto, Pilgrims, and Wampanoag today. We honor them because of events long ago.
- Basic needs are the same now as in the past, but the ways we meet them are different.
- How to identify land and water on the globe and map.

- Identify differences between needs and wants.
- Dramatize life from long ago.
- Identify Squanto, Pilgrims, and Wampanoag
- Identify food, shelter, and clothing from long ago and now.
- Locate land and water on the map and globe.

STAGE 2—ASSESSMENT EVIDENCE

Performance Tasks
- Through role playing students will show their understanding of people and events of long ago and how people met their basic needs.
- Children will create a mural illustrating life from long ago.
- Children will create a classroom dramatization of Wampanoag life and take on various roles within a story (Pilgrim life/Wampanoag life). Their goal is to teach another kindergarten class about life long ago. Each student will depict how basic needs of life long ago were met (transportation, shelter, food, and survival). The audience will participate in a conversation with the actors after the presentation is over.

Other Evidence
- Interview: Tell me the story of the first Thanksgiving. Use of follow-up questions and discussion.
- Interview: Tell me about life long ago vs. life today.
- Anecdotal records.
- Movement and role playing that show how the Pilgrims and Wampanoag met their basic needs.
- Journal entries: drawings/writings with oral comments.
- Drawings, paintings, costumes, and miniature 3–D replicas.
- Revisions on graphic organizers such as wants and needs.

STAGE 3—LEARNING PLAN

- Identify people and events from long, long ago.
- Hook children on role playing people and events by creating with them a long-ago center where children can reenact Pilgrim and Wampanoag life.
- Hook by making connections between their families' immigration and the Pilgrims' immigration.
- Equip children by teaching mini-lessons on how to use pictures from nonfiction books to get information, how to listen and ask questions during read-alouds, and how to use the body to communicate.
- Use and add on to Venn diagrams, T-charts, and concept maps as graphic organizers to help children compare and contrast basic needs of life long ago and today.
- Evaluate children through discussion, interviews, art, movement, role playing, and writing.
- Tailor learning by working in small groups, bringing in antiques, making replicas for the museum in progress.
- Organize the learning by ongoing assessment of their growing understanding of life long ago.

Key Activities

- Children will create a family photo album to understand that we are all immigrants coming to the United States, using their families' home countries and reasons they came to the United States. We want children to link this to the Pilgrims and how they left England to come to America.
- Children will go to the computer lab and use the smart board with an interactive map
  - To identify their country and its proximity to the United States.
  - To trace the voyage of the Mayflower.
- Children will draw the shape of their country using Kid Pix.
- Children will use flags to graph their home country and home language.
- Mini-lessons to teach vocabulary of long ago and Pilgrims/Wampanoags
  - How to learn from nonfiction texts (Kate Waters), realia, photographs, and Web sites
- Virtual tour of Plimoth Plantation http://www.plimoth.org/visit/virtual/
  - Gather objects from nature to build a longhouse, campfires, fishing nets, canoes, and Pilgrim buildings.
  - Role play and movement showing scenes from long-ago environment (coming to America, hunting, gardening, etc.)
  - Venn Diagram comparing basic needs from long ago and now.
  - Sort pictures from now and long ago.
  - Sort pictures based on wants and needs.
  - Dance a Story: The Brave Indian. This story reinforces through movement how Native Americans grew into warriors who hunted food for their villages. Includes "becoming" the hunter, the weather surrounding the village, and creatures in the forest on the hunt.
  - Children learn to sing and play historical singing games, such as Here We Go Round the Mulberry Bush to learn about daily actions of early Americans and Wind the Wool to learn how wool was wound into yarn. (We "wind" ourselves into a ball.)

RUBRIC

Trait	Early Emergent	Developing Emergent	Emergent	Novice
Vocabulary/ terminology	Child's actions don't match the words.	Has a partial understanding of terminology needed to express ideas.	Has a substantial understanding of terminology needed to express ideas.	Has a thorough understanding of terminology needed to express ideas.
Time	Has serious misconceptions when comparing long ago and now.	Has partial understanding when comparing long ago and now.	Has substantial understanding when comparing long ago and now.	Has a thorough understanding when comparing long ago and now.
Nonfiction/ drawing	Shows misunderstanding of events and basic needs.	Shows some understanding of events and basic needs.	Shows generally accurate understanding of events and basic needs.	Shows completely accurate understanding of events and basic needs.

		RUBRIC *(continued)*		
Drama	Ineffective in using imagination to role play characters from another time.	Somewhat effective in using imagination to role play characters from another time.	Generally effective in using imagination to role play characters from another time.	Highly effective in using imagination to role play characters from another time.
Visual	Ineffective in demonstrating daily life of long ago through different media.	Somewhat effective in demonstrating daily life of long ago through different media.	Generally effective in demonstrating daily life of long ago through different media.	Highly effective in demonstrating daily life of long ago through different media.

Implementing Hands-on Learning Plans

The hands-on learning activities for any unit start with research: asking and answering questions as we read and look at books, posters, and Web sites. The classes involved in this unit work hard to establish areas of the classroom that look like the visual images they have studied. The children paint a mural for their Pilgrim house. In the dramatic play area, they turn around the existing parts of the area that do not represent long ago. Together we cover the backs of the sink, refrigerator, and stove with brown paper on which the children paint a mural of an ocean and garden for the backdrop as we design our Pilgrim cooking area. We pore over the photographs in the books by Kate Waters: *Samuel Eaton's Day, Tapenum's Day, On the Mayflower,* and *Sarah Morton's Day.*

Together we add wood for the fire, a cast-iron pot, antique utensils, a large cloth stuffed with straw to sleep on, and slate for writing. We find clamshells, plant pumpkin seeds, grind corn, sew burlap into pockets, and sew poppet dolls. Children cuddle up with fur from animals; make hats to wear in the hot sun as they garden; dress up in clothes from long ago; rest on a wooden bench; and create traps, bows, arrows, and nets for surviving long, long ago. The children refer to texts repeatedly to make their replicas as accurate as possible.

Students solve many problems as they search for just the right sticks outside to make a grate to go over the fire or a stick that bends to make a trap to catch animals. They make clay pots. They cart mulch, rocks, sticks, and straw into the classroom to make thatch houses and longhouses. They pretend to catch fish, to hunt for deer, and to care for the sick without a doctor. They cook meals and plant the crops. (See Figures 6.2 and 6.3.)

Figures 6.2 and 6.3 Housekeeping centers in each kindergarten room evolve into different aspects of long ago. Jenrry and Michelle lead their Native American crew on a fishing expedition. When their class visits another classroom, the crew will have an opportunity to play in a longhouse.

Daily we read new books on the Pilgrims and the Wampanoag. The new vocabulary and new information enrich the play in the Long-Ago center, which has been turned into a living museum. As the children learn new words, they label those parts of their museum: straw bed, fire, slate board, Atlantic Ocean, and so on. Children write about long, long ago during writing workshop time. As we mentioned earlier, we do not assign topics to children during writing workshops. However, we do show them how to write nonfiction. They learn that authors have to check their facts and make sure they are accurate. The students learn to label drawings and write short pieces about living long ago. When writing nonfiction, children learn to think of their audience and what is important for their audience to understand. Thus, learning to both read and write nonfiction is integrated into the language arts time as the children delve into the latest social studies topics.

One of the keys to the success of any social studies unit for second language learners is that the children learn from each other. They often return to text written by classmates or to displays. Classes visit other classrooms to see what they are learning. In the case of the change-over-time unit discussed previously, these mini field trips to other classrooms enable children to explore canoes, longhouses, the Mayflower, Plimoth Plantation, a Wampanoag village, and children's games from the period. Children develop a deeper understanding of long ago as they learn from each classroom museum they visit.

They slowly learn the vocabulary and the purposes of the items in the area as they use them. The books stay in the area to refer to as they play. Before they have "free play" in the area during free choice time, an adult meets with children in small groups. As they stand at the door of Plimoth Plantation, the children and the adult quietly go back in time. After entering the area, they all participate in pretend play. "It is night time. I am hungry. What shall we eat? How shall we cook it?" Their long-ago dramatic play includes learning to hunt for deer, to cook on the outdoor stove, and to light candles to see. As the adult feels the children have enough language and concepts to use the language and artifacts from long ago, the adult steps out of the pretend play. Children are encouraged to stay in character during their time in the Long-Ago area.

One year an extremely active boy, Gabriel, was particularly interested in why so many of the Pilgrims died. He often acted out that part in the center. His classmates would minister to his needs to no avail. He would announce that he did not have enough food, it was too cold, and that he did not know about germs and would die. We watched in amazement as he kept his body still for an extended length of time as he gradually "died." The children would sadly announce, "Gabriel's dying." Before long, he would come to life and prepare to die all over again!

We have a feast day when each class cooks authentic dishes from long, long ago to share with the entire grade level. We make costumes, share our meal together, and then spend time traveling from room to room learning from each classroom museum. This emphasis on visual images, drama, and games during social studies time helps ELLs get through the layers of meaning in the content.

Social studies is also often integrated into other areas of the curriculum. During physical education children enjoy outdoor games of the past such as hoops, marbles, and hopscotch. The performing arts teacher, Carmen Boatwright-Bacon, teaches the children how to act out a hunting story from the point of view of a Wampanoag boy. The art teacher, Dania Abimourched, instructs the children in pottery making just as the people long ago would have done.

Change over time and the past are very difficult concepts for young children. Through active learning the students begin to internalize the information, and they will use this learning as hooks for making connections through the upcoming years, as they tackle other social studies objectives, such as famous people. George Washington, Abraham Lincoln, John Chapman, Martin Luther King, Jr., and others take their place in history based on children's understandings from the first unit.

For example, Gabriel continued to be fascinated with death. He was always curious about how George Washington, Abraham Lincoln, Martin Luther King, Jr., and other famous people died. He would always ask the question, "Did he die?" when we talked about a person. Even when we did author studies of Audrey and Don Wood or Robert Munsch, his question popped up. We referred to time lines to assure him they were not dead. Gabriel was trying to master the concept of past and present. Death was his way of dealing with it. Past and present is a concept that young children mature into slowly. One way we know that it takes time to master this concept is a question we always get: "Did Abraham Lincoln know Martin Luther King?"

Sometimes we plan to revisit social studies vocabulary, and sometimes there are teachable moments that give us the opportunity to review. We use these opportunities to refer to difficult vocabulary and concepts throughout the year.

- To keep the learning alive, we put pictures of the activities on the screen-saver slide show. The children love to gather around the computer and chat as pictures from our units pop on and off the screen. It is refreshing to hear them still use the vocabulary months later.
- Together children reread class Big Books made with the pictures. They never tire of seeing pictures of themselves dressed in costume or working on a project.
- As part of the change-over-time unit, in November the children took home their pumpkin plants that had been started in little egg shells. A delightful teachable moment for review arose before spring break during writing workshop. Sarah started writing about her pumpkin plant again. (See Figure 6.4.) Her plant had started to bloom at home. She brought

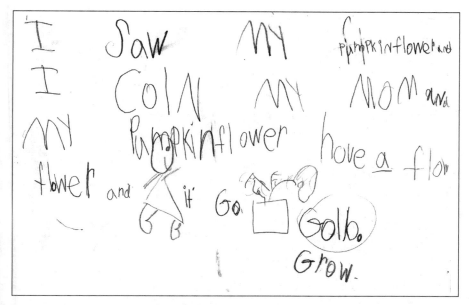

Figure 6.4 Sarah's story about her pumpkin plant. (I saw my pumpkin flower and I called my Mom and my pumpkin flower have a flower and it grow gold.)

it back in to show us that the pumpkin vine now had flowers. The class reviewed the life cycle of a pumpkin plant from science as well as how the Pilgrims and Wampanoag grew all their food. The next day during writing workshop she put this all together in a how-to book. (See Figure 6.5.)

Engaging Students in Hands-on Learning and Skills

The simple activity of spinning a globe at the beginning of a unit enabled all children to participate and understand the lesson. Each child enjoyed stopping the spinning globe with his or her finger and calling out, "Land!" or "Water!" We tallied the times we landed on water or land, and the class concluded that most of the earth is water. This helped the children realize that the Pilgrims came across a great deal of water on a small boat for a long time. As the unit progressed, students marked their country of origin on the globe or on maps. The children would announce how their family got to America if they knew. If not, their homework was to go home and conduct research by interviewing family members on how their family came to America: by land, water, or sky.

One morning the electricity went off in the building. We could imagine teachers at every grade level pausing to talk about life long ago. How did people know what time it was? How did they eat? Read? Cook? Stories told

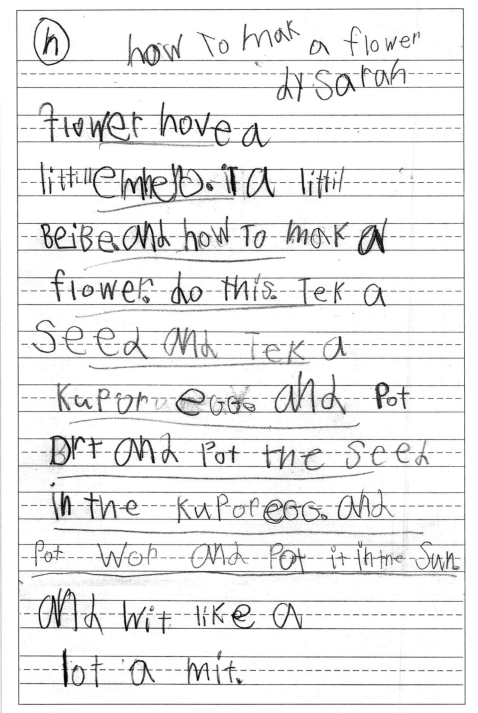

ⓗ   how To mak a flower
                    by sarah
flower hove a
littill embeyo. it a littil
beibe and how To mak a
flower. do this. Tek a
seed and Tek a
Kupor egg and Pot
Drt and Pot the seed
in the Kupor egg. and
Pot Wot and Pot it in the Sun
and wit like a
lot a mit.

Figure 6.5 Sarah's how-to book. (How to make a flower by Sarah. Flower have a little embryo. It a little baby. And how to make a flower. Do this. Take a seed and take a cup or egg. And put dirt and put the seed in the cup or egg. And put water and put it in the sun. And wait like a lot a minute.)

sitting on the floor around a candle stick or a pretend fire took place in many rooms as other lessons were temporarily halted for this teachable moment.

Other teachable moments arise throughout the day when we make connections to other countries, such as Vietnam, Mexico, England, or Cambodia, because of an object, a story, or a news item from that country. We find the country on a map or globe and see where it is in relationship to America and to their families' countries of origin.

We put colored tape on the floor to outline the continents and oceans so that young children can pretend to go from one land to another. When the children complement their drama with facial expressions of anticipation, fear, and anxiety, we know their understanding is developing.

The children also enjoy acting out the planting, harvesting, cooking, hunting, building, sewing, mucking, and all manner of chores. They also might have an opportunity to watch their older cousins, siblings, or friends in another grade giving a dramatic presentation about the Underground Railroad. Drama is used across the grade levels at our school to help students to a deeper level of understanding and is an important door to understanding abstract concepts for our ELLs.

Storytelling and story retelling are an integral part of the language arts curricula. During social studies units, storytelling "through the mask" is an effective technique for teaching content or letting others know what you have learned. Storytelling through a mask is adaptable for any concept: I am a cloud, I am the flag, I am a magnet, or I am a rock. A mentor book that shows this well is *Atlantic* by G. Brian Karas. It begins, "I am the Atlantic Ocean. I begin where the land runs out at the end of yards and streets and hills." After telling their stories, children can write them into books for sharing with other classes or for reading to other members of their own class. (To learn more about writing through a mask refer to *Craft Lessons* by Ralph Fletcher and JoAnn Portalupi.)

Books by Kate Waters, such as *Sarah Morton's Day*, *Samuel Eaton's Day*, and *Tapenum's Day*, are good examples of first-person or through-the-mask storytelling for young students. We use these books and her Web site to teach the children throughout the unit. The children then learn to speak in the first person as if they are Sarah, Samuel, or Tapenum. As they tell their stories in dramatic play, we discover what they know. They solidify their learning and share with others. We are teaching them skills they will use throughout the grade levels to portray their learning.

They also learn to write these stories during writing workshop through the mask of these characters. They learn that storytellers such as Robert Munsch do not write down their stories until they have perfected them in front of multiple audiences. One of the children's favorite books is a story by Robert Munsch called *From Far Away*. It is about Saoussan, who comes to

Canada from war-torn Beirut in kindergarten and does not know any English. She tells her story as a third grader in letters to Robert Munsch, a Canadian storyteller and author. He in turn tells the story from behind the mask of this child. Using Robert Munsch as a mentor author, children learn to tell their stories. Children can learn to use drama to tell their stories at an early age, and with little English. After they have performed their stories, they can then focus on writing them down.

We also integrate science objectives about living things into our social studies units. As a learning activity, children plant seeds and learn about life cycles of plants. We plant pumpkin seeds and corn seeds. Children learn their seeds will not sprout or their plants will not thrive if they do not water them. This practice of learning about plants during social studies continues throughout the grade levels. As children learn about our state history or Native Americans, they will be involved in planting herbs or cooking foods they are studying in the unit.

Other hands-on activities include gathering straw and sticks to make replicas of thatched roof houses and fences, sewing pockets, eating cranberries without sugar, or preparing corn in a variety of ways. Children learn to use this information in their dramatic play. Likewise, they will continue these types of activities as they learn in later years about Ancient Egypt, slavery, or Colonial America. Hands-on learning and integration of science, math, reading, and writing into lessons throughout the grade levels are a way to help ELLs grasp complex issues and information. Children's learning in all grade levels is represented in the small museums that fill our hallways and rooms. Thus, children are exposed to the upper-grade social studies content long before they actually study it.

Assessing Children During Social Studies

Observing children during drama is a means of ongoing assessment. If they are not acting out a scene with accuracy, we know it is time to bring out the books and look at more pictures to clarify any misunderstanding. Interviewing children as we proceed in the unit always reveals new things about their learning and our teaching. We use this information to help us reteach (material/information/a skill) or to clarify or enhance a child's understanding. When we have asked the essential questions at the end of a unit, we have often found they are difficult for ELLs to answer. We solve this problem by rewording the question until the child understands what we mean.

For example, Emelie asked, "Eliza, how do people today and in the past meet their basic needs?" Eliza looked at her blankly.

"Are the basic needs the same now as a long time ago?" Another blank look.

Emelie asked again, "Eliza, think about long, long ago. What did the people need?"

"Water and food."

"Do people need water and food today?"

"Yes."

"What else do people need?"

"I need a doctor."

"Did they need a doctor long ago?"

Catching on, Eliza says quickly, "Yes. No doctors! They died. They make a house. I have a house."

From this interchange we recognize that Eliza knows that people of all times need water, food, and shelter. We know that she understands that the people had basic needs but were lacking in some areas, such as medical care. From this little assessment the teacher can build on what Eliza knows and develop her vocabulary and content knowledge. For example, Eliza will benefit from exploring more picture books that contrast the past and present for gathering and preparing food. Playing with her friends in pretend centers will help her learn to use the vocabulary. Her language development and understanding of the social studies content would be noted on our division's assessment rubric.

Involving Parents in Social Studies Learning

The change-over-time unit we have used as an example in this chapter was also introduced in Emelie's class to the parents. This was done in the morning during the Parents as Teachers time using nonfiction books. The parents started talking with their children about how so many of the pictures looked like their own countries with the cooking, the houses, and the gardens. It was a way for the parents to make connections to our learning and to learn some American history and a way for the children to understand that part of American history is the "coming-to-America" story. Hearing parents telling these short stories was also a good introduction to storytelling. In order to learn to tell stories, children need to hear others tell stories, and we try to use every available opportunity to make this possible.

Part of our state's social studies standards call for children to recognize "that communities in Virginia include people who have diverse ethnic origins, customs and traditions that make contributions to their communities and who are united as Americans by common principles" (Commonwealth of Virginia Board of Education 2001).

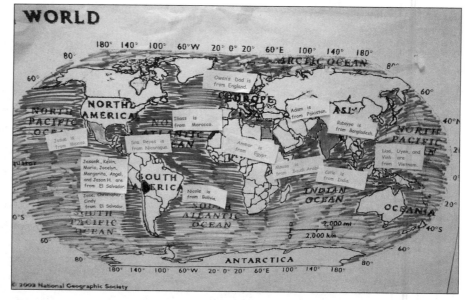

Figure 6.6 In this hallway map, the children and parents can read the simple patterned text, "Iliass is from Morocco."

The first day of the Long Ago unit, eight parents were in the class working with their children during Parents as Teachers time. We invited them to stay longer for our social studies lesson. The parents showed us where they came from on the map and told us why they came to America. One of the parents acted as an interpreter. We put a sticker on each country on the map and listed reasons they came: for education, for a job, for religion, for safety, for a better life for their children.

To start our study we showed the parents and children on the map where the Pilgrims came from and told them we were going to learn about when the Pilgrims came to America and why they came. In this sharing of coming-to-America stories, parents help children understand the reasons behind the Pilgrims' journey.

Classes at Bailey's often place large maps outside their rooms. Parents help their children find their country of origin. Children sometimes place their pictures around the outside of the map and stretch yarn linking them to their countries or choose to show the connection in other ways. Parents gather around these maps and chat in their native language about the children and their homes. (See Figure 6.6.)

Parents often come to the classes and talk about their country. A wonderful part of teaching in a school where there are ELLs is the use of rich family stories to enhance our learning. (See Figure 6.7.)

This year Tess had the opportunity to teach a short unit called Coming to America with Leisha Lawrence's first-grade class. Leisha wanted to pro-

Figure 6.7 Rohan's mother visits Christine Sganga's classroom to talk about Rohan's homeland of India.

vide an opportunity for the students to work with nonfiction text. Using informational sources is a language arts standard that is required in first grade.

This is a wonderful unit to teach in our school because it develops so naturally and is of such high interest to all our students, whatever their level of English. We can comfortably integrate the learning standards about past and present, geography, economics, and language arts from the first-grade curriculum in very visual ways that make it easier for our ELLs to participate more fully.

Leisha's students were familiar with the Pilgrims' experiences as they came to this country, so they had some historical context about leaving one country in order to travel to another. They also knew their own families' experiences. The idea of diverse origins is something we talk about all year long. Our students' and teachers' personal connections to stories and events are often prefaced with, "In my country . . ." The children respond with genuine interest and respect to such openings.

On this occasion Tess brought in a pile of library books about her native England. She used the illustrations to highlight some of the main features of life in England. The children were deeply interested and asked all sorts of questions about the red buses, the Queen and her palace, the school uniforms, and so on. After talking for a while Tess paired the children so that each ELL was partnered with a fluent English speaker. She gave each pair one of the books and asked them to spread out and spend about five minutes to find something interesting about England in their book. Back in the circle they shared the pictures that had caught their attention. Jeyson pointed at a picture and smiled shyly, whereas Thahn talked comfortably about her picture. Both were acceptable ways to share.

Tess then asked them to tell her which countries their families came from. Honduras, Vietnam, Guatemala, Cuba, France, Italy, El Salvador, Wisconsin, Virginia, came the answers. "Wouldn't it be interesting to find out about all these countries or states?" asked Tess, as she slowly spun the globe next to her. "I wonder how we could do that." "We can get more books from the library," suggested Idan. "We can look on the computer," said John. So Tess agreed that she would return the next day with books about all their countries.

The next day Tess grouped the children by their countries and gave them an opportunity to look at the books. Tess and Leisha sat with the ELLs, who were now grouped together, to help them understand their books, although this was hardly necessary. They were excited to see pictures of things they recognized. Later the students would decide on the most important facts to know about a country in order to create a pictorial data-retrieval chart. Thus, Alberto was able to add a picture of his mom's Cuban chicken dish; Jeyson was able to enlist Leisha's help to print a picture of money from El Salvador; Thahn was able to draw a picture of people planting rice; and Willie could add a picture of the Wisconsin state flag. Leisha added photos of the children to a large world map that Tess had prepared with the children as they learned the names of oceans and continents. This brief study culminated with a class potluck for which several children brought in a native dish to share.

In past years, Tess has also celebrated with a family bookmaking night to draw the unit to a close. Parents and grandparents enjoyed looking at the books of their countries. They told stories to the children as they worked together to illustrate and write in the blank books Tess had prepared. Tess had videotaped throughout the project, and once the bookmaking evening was added to the tape, she was able to send it home for families to view.

Planning Bilingual Lessons

We know bilingual lessons are powerful. We have many bilingual books in our rooms as well as books in children's home languages. We wish we were multilingual so that we could talk to all our children in their home languages. However, we both only speak English. We take an upset child by the hand to have Chau Nguyen, our Vietnamese school secretary, explain to her that when she brings her library books back, she can check out another one. We will ask the cafeteria manager, Fadwa Sarsaur, to speak Arabic to a little boy explaining to him that we want him to bring his parents back to the school that night for Family Learning Night. In other words, we will use home languages when we can.

Occasionally we have a lesson that we do in two languages. We have many Spanish bilingual staff members and some dual-language and Spanish-immersion classes. One example of a bilingual lesson is a social studies lesson on Dr. Martin Luther King, Jr.

It was important for parents and students to understand why we were going to have a Monday holiday. We wanted them to understand this part of American history. Sra. Ada Prabhabvat teaches Spanish Immersion in first grade. When her students arrived Friday morning, she brought them down the hall to the kindergarten classroom to sit on the floor with the younger students. Around the outside sat parents who had walked their children to school.

The children got very quiet. This was a different way to start the day. Something important was happening. As Emelie read David Adler's *A Picture Book of Martin Luther King Jr*, Ada taught the lesson with her in Spanish. We told the parents and students the story of the life of Dr. Martin Luther King, Jr. We used pictures, poems, and songs. The students and parents joined in with us on the repetitive parts of the poems.

What a beautiful lesson for forty-five children who were not being "judged by the color of their skin" but were snuggling close to each other on a rug, learning together! Trini's mother sat close to her daughter during the lesson. She whispered the lesson in Vietnamese into her daughter's ear to make sure she understood.

We wondered what the parents were thinking as they listened intently. Most of these parents had not been to school in their own country at all or perhaps had attended for just a few years. We hoped they were making connections with their own lives and would continue talking about it over dinner that night with their children.

This lesson was at 8:40 in the morning. Later on in the day, Gabriel was walking around hugging a picture of Dr. King saying to others, "I miss him. I miss him." Walking out to recess, Nancy asked, "When you were a little girl, was your skin black?" Bruce Lee found the book and picture depicting the assassination. He asked, "Did the man with hate in his heart have white skin?" Our hope was that these thoughts and persistent questions would linger in their heads all weekend and that, as they saw Martin Luther King, Jr., on television, they would have conversations as a family about him and other people who have made a difference in their lives.

Making Abstract Concepts Concrete

So much of social studies is abstract learning. We know that making abstract social studies concepts as concrete as possible helps the ELL. We attempt to do that through developing lessons that make history come alive for the students and by integrating it into science and math, as well as language arts. For example when studying the many aspects of community, the children help turn the dramatic play area into a post office and the writing center into a card shop, and the coins and scales come out in the math and science area. All this is in preparation for a walking field trip to tour the post office.

We go in the morning while the mail carriers are still at their stations loading the mail. Some children get to see their carrier and their box. Each child writes a letter to a family member, addresses an envelope, and counts out the correct change to take along to buy a stamp.

We step over melting snow, clutch our envelopes and bags of coins, and wiggle with anticipation as we enter our neighborhood post office. Once inside we watch workers weigh, sort, and ship packages. We go out to the loading dock to see how the trucks are loaded. A highlight is watching the big mail-sorting machines and the carriers sort mail into each house's slot. We buy stamps, mail our letters, and walk back to school.

Before and after the trip the children practice wrapping and weighing packages, writing letters, buying and selling cards and stamps, and delivering letters to friends in and out of our room. Children learn about the development of the postal service over time through picture books. The experience of entering the lobby of the post office is a first for many children. The experience of going into the back room of the post office is a first for all the children and their parents. The words: *post office*, *mail carrier*, *packages*, *stamp*, and *services* now have concrete meaning for the students.

We take many pictures on digital cameras during a field trip. After printing them, children each choose one to write about during writing workshop. Soon we have a class book about the day. Children are learning to write nonfiction during social studies. Later on, families can see the laminated pages displayed in the post-office lobby. We also put the pictures on the screen-saver slide show of the computer along with pictures of other units of study we have enjoyed. The children review the vocabulary and what they have learned every time they see the pictures.

Teaching Social Studies All Day

Throughout the day, the children learn about civics objectives. We teach good citizenship through our daily experiences in the classroom and school community. As mentioned in our chapter on building community, class meetings are a powerful vehicle for teaching children what it means to "Respect yourself. Respect others. Respect school property." Civics objectives in our first-grade curriculum state that children will apply the trait of good citizenship by focusing on fair play, exhibiting good sportsmanship, helping others, treating others with respect, recognizing the purpose of rules and practicing self-control, working hard in school, taking responsibility for one's own actions, and valuing honesty and truthfulness in oneself and others.

For children who are learning to communicate in a second language, these objectives are very abstract. How can a child in the early production stage of English acquisition follow the teacher's direction to "use your words" to show how he or she feels? As the class works together to solve problems during our class meetings, however, the children come to understand the meanings of respect, honesty, truthfulness, self-control, responsibility, and so on. With practice, a child can learn to say, "I feel sad when you . . ."

Children learn how to listen, use connective language, and solve problems together through these class meetings. During the first few meetings, the children learn how to give compliments. "Thank you Juruvith for helping me clean up the paint when I spilled it."

After learning about compliments, the children decide on their class rules. Children and teachers set expectations for what they want their class to be like. They review them at subsequent meetings and talk about key words and body language to use in day-to-day problem-solving and discussions. Children learn to use connective language as they solve problems. "I agree with Xavier that two people are enough for the block center." Or "I disagree with Xavier. I think four children are better."

It takes the first week for a class to agree on behaviors and then to summarize them into just a few rules. One year a class might decide that all their rules can be summarized in this way: "Listen to everyone. Be kind to everyone. Use words to solve problems." Another year the class might decide that just the word *respect* is enough. (For more on developing class rules, see *Rules in School* by Northeast Foundation Center.)

In class meetings, teachers and children bring up issues related to good citizenship. Children brainstorm ways to solve problems and then practice the solutions. If a child is running around the room, the class works on a solution. They practice using words: "I feel scared when you run around because I think I'll get hurt." They also practice extending their arm and hand in a stop sign when children are bothering them. Finally, they practice moving away if the first steps do not work.

Children with little oral or receptive language at the beginning of the year are still able to understand enough of these first lessons to know what is going on because the class acts out the problem and the solution. We give our ELLs the language they need and time to practice using it during role playing. This helps children learn what it means to be a contributing member of a democratic society. As we have already mentioned, Dr. Nelson's book *Positive Discipline in the Classroom* is a good reference for class meetings.

For children who are just learning English, we keep in mind that proficiency in oral and written English does not keep children from learning social studies or any content area. We cannot wait for children to be proficient in English before beginning to teach content. Virginia Collier cites much research, including her own, to suggest that it takes a minimum of seven to ten years to acquire academic language and one to three for social language (1995). We must make the information accessible to ELLs at every stage of English proficiency. We can aid them in learning by planning lessons that will access students' prior knowledge, use hands-on learning as much as possible, teach strategies to read the many types of nonfiction text, integrate the content throughout the day, and provide alternative means of assessing their learning.

MATH
WORKSHOP

The numerous difficulties ESL students can expect to experience in math, apart from making simple computational errors, suggests that special procedures are needed that enable students to test hypotheses about language use and other potential problem areas. One such procedure is cooperative work activities in which students discuss their interpretation of a problem, identify steps that are necessary to find the solution, test out different approaches, and check their answers relative to solutions obtained by other students.

Anna Uhl Chamot and J. Michael O'Malley, *The CALLA Handbook*

When we think back to the first math lessons of any year, we remember how overwhelming it always is to see the wide range of students' English acquisition as well as their math ability. The range of abilities that we observe during September's free exploration time causes us to pause. There is the one student who is able to count money, count by twos, count backwards, add and subtract mentally; knows the names of shapes and their attributes; and can make complex patterns. Then there are too many who cannot yet count to two, recognize any numbers or shapes in their first language or in English, or copy a simple red-blue pattern. Some know how to count to ten in their language but not in English. Some know names of shapes or colors in their language but not in English. We recall that overwhelming feeling of wondering where to start. How can we possibly meet all their needs?

Emelie remembers walking around one fall assessing the children on seriation as they made balls with clay. Kaylin was stacking together various sizes of clay. Looking up at her teacher she smiled, "Pancake for party!" Emelie sat down and started chatting with Kaylin as she molded a couple more flat discs. As Kaylin carefully made each one just a little smaller and continued to stack them, Emelie exclaimed, "Oh, you are making a birthday cake for a party!" Kaylin beamed because she knew that her teacher understood her. Emelie knew that Kaylin could seriate and was at either the early production or speech emergence stage of language development. Equally important was that Kaylin knew if she took risks with her language, her teacher would try to understand her.

Erick sat silently next to Kaylin, happily stacking his clay discs any which way. Emelie's assessment of Erick was that as a Spanish speaker at a preproductive stage of English development, Erick was content to follow directions by watching the other children, could not yet seriate, and was storing words for the future.

Observations like these make us realize how wasteful it would be for Kaylin to spend days learning to seriate sizes just because Erick could not. We sigh deeply, knowing that we are not going to spend a week on seriating, the number one, the color red, or shapes because it would be wasted time for some children. We know our job is to find out what each child knows and to teach children what they need. We differentiate for math as we do for language arts. We know we have the whole year for the children to learn at their own speed, starting with where they are that day.

Teaching arithmetic to English language learners (how to add, subtract, multiply, and divide) is much easier than teaching them mathematics (problem-solving by thinking and reasoning mathematically). We want the children to learn arithmetic well, but we need them to use their basic facts, estimation, and arithmetic processes not in isolation but in problem-solving situations.

It is difficult for ELLs to problem-solve with money, fractions, and measurement, for example, because of the immense amount of language required. It is challenging to teach both arithmetic and mathematics well to all children; however, it is essential that all children learn to use mathematics in purposeful ways. We want them to be flexible in their thinking. We want them to develop techniques and skills necessary to use mental math and alternative algorithms in their everyday world.

Often people will say to us, "I'm sure being an English language learner is less of an issue in math than in any other subject area." That really is a misconception. Language is critical in arithmetic and mathematics. Knowing and using math language is often the key to solving math problems. Students must first understand what actions are taking place in a problem, as well as what the problem is asking. When children have limited English, the teacher has the challenge of teaching not only math concepts and problem-solving skills but also the social, concept, and academic language of math as well.

Let's look at an example: Maria saw two dogs, three birds, and one duck at the park. How many animals did she see in all? The teacher may need to introduce new vocabulary or connect the animal vocabulary to students' science or language arts study. Additionally, the teacher needs to assess whether or not the ELLs understand the academic language, such as *how many* and *in all*. Finally, when the students have an understanding of what question the problem is asking, they can move on to using their arithmetic skills to solve the problem.

We have to design math lessons in which all children can be successful as they problem-solve. In order to do this, teachers must do much more than teach the math skills and concepts. Students must learn language to make math meaningful.

Integrating Math into Daily Routines and Other Content Areas

We learn to speak by using oral language structures and vocabulary in context. The context frames the meaning and purpose that drives our acquisition of language. Therefore, we need to create contexts in which the language of math can be meaningful and purposeful for our students. We seize opportunities to teach, practice, and learn math all day.

When we line up, we are learning math concepts and vocabulary.

"Two children line up on the red line. Thank you. Now will two more children line up on the green line please? Next, we need four children on the yellow line. Who can tell us what we need to do to make the lines equal?" After determining which line has the most children and which the least, we are almost ready to go. As we leave class, we practice the difficult ordinal numbers and position words.

"Today we will have the red line go first. I see that the green line is ready. They can go second. Yellow line, you can be third today. Remember the last group has to close the door."

Many daily routines are constant ways children can learn that math is always around them: practice with the calendar, weather, or temperature graphs; counting how many people are at school and how many are absent; counting to the 100th day; or counting down to important days and holidays.

Every time we draw an animal or object, we talk about which shape to use. "The giraffe has a long rectangle for the neck. What shapes should we use for the head and ears?"

This constant reinforcement of math vocabulary and concepts is important for ELLs. We know that studying shapes for a week will not put the language into a child's long-term memory. We revisit the names of shapes often in many contexts.

We embed math language and concepts in lessons throughout the year. On the first day of school, we graph not only boys and girls but also walkers, bus riders, and car riders, and which languages children can speak. We use pictures to illustrate each of these so that children with very limited English feel comfortable participating in the graphing. Throughout the year students learn math language and concepts as they move, sing songs, or enjoy exploring literature. A book such as *Rosie's Walk*, by Pat Hutchins, is a wonderful way to learn concepts such as next to, around, over, under, and through. (See Figure 7.1.)

During an economics unit, a class produces a product and sells it to students from other classes using real money. Children enjoy honing their money skills so they can work in the hallway marketplace booths selling popcorn, plants, play dough, or stationery.

To learn the concepts behind certain language we integrate geometry and measurement into science lessons or social studies lessons where it is applicable. Measuring plant growth, the garden plot, or measuring the length of the Mayflower puts meaning behind the language.

Choosing Math Activities During Free-Choice Learning Centers

Children choose activities during free-choice learning centers that involve math learning. Many love clipboards and enjoy using their English to gather

Figure 7.1 Mary Anne Buckley makes good use of her digital camera to illustrate kindergarten class books. This picture of Nestor will become part of a book illustrating words such as *under, over, next to,* or *through.*

data in and out of the classroom. They can ask the same question repeatedly in the hallway, in the cafeteria, or in other classes. Often they will pair up with children who are more confident in their English speaking. After preparing their clipboards with a question and columns for tallying answers, the students practice the question in the safety of the classroom with a few classmates. Then off they go together out into the school to gather data. (See Figure 7.2.)

Sample questions that children use in their surveys are:

- Which is your favorite zoo animal?
  horse pig zebra snake monkey
- Who is your favorite author?
  Audrey and Don Wood   Leo Leonni   Eric Carle
- What is your favorite season?
  summer fall winter spring
- What did you do on the snow day?
  watch TV sled read

Students return with tally marks and show their clipboards with delight. The students are encouraged to make a graph to share the data with the class. After sharing their results, the children display their graphs in the hall-way for the rest of the school to see. While collecting data, making tally

Figure 7.2 Teachers cheerfully accept interruptions when students come to ask survey questions. Jon Leavitt listens as Max takes his turn asking the question, while his friends record the answer.

marks, recording data on a graph, writing about the results, and speaking in front of strangers, children are using English for a purpose.

Money in the drama center gives children the opportunity to use a cash register and recognize the names of the coins and their values. It allows them the opportunity to practice the language of shopping. Encouraging the children to set up a grocery store, post office, card shop, or bookstore gives the children time to practice with money at their level of expertise. They enjoy putting price tags on their works of art and "selling" them. If an adult, or a child who has mastered money, is playing in the center, it ensures that the children are using correct terms for the coins.

Water table, rice table, sand table, balance scales, tape measures, and rulers are favorites for young children during free-choice time. Beakers, funnels, measuring cups, spoons, and a box full of items to weigh and measure will lead to children discovering and practicing volume, capacity, weight, and length. At class meetings, the class decides how many children should be at this center at a time. Usually they decide three is the correct number for water, rice, or sand, or it will end up on the floor. We also have added sand and water tables to our outside science lab, where small groups of children can experiment without worrying about spills.

At any center we prefer a proficient English speaker to be playing with a limited English speaker. If this is not possible, we briefly stop by to comment on what is happening. As we chat, we use the concept words repeatedly. "Look at you pouring the rice from the large beaker to the smaller beaker! Which one holds more rice? What happens when you pour from the small beaker to the larger beaker? How many times do you have to pour it? Do you pour two times? Do you pour three times?" If the students are using links, paper clips, or rulers to measure length, we say "Line up your measuring tool along the edge," reinforcing important words. These brief conversations remind students of the language of that center.

Leaving the counters and other manipulatives out for the children to use during free play is helpful. A toy airplane that was a counter now becomes an active part of pretend play. This way the social, labeling, and content vocabulary increases through play.

Pattern blocks, attribute blocks, Legos, and wooden blocks are also favorite choices during learning centers. Children extend their math learning during play when they ask for a rectangular prism or a rhombus as they build constructions. Often we hear questions like, "Teacher! Come look. Is this symmetrical?" Or a child's voice will joyfully ring out, "We made a pattern!" Their play is rich in both language and math learning.

Another very popular station is the teacher station. Children will use the large dry-erase board, the calendar, and games surrounding the teacher station as they play. Because their teachers speak English, they will use English and mimic the phrases and sentences they have heard. "One, two, three, look at me. Tell me the number that you see." The child pretending to be the teacher will flash a dot card for the students sitting in front of the rocking chair. Sometimes the students will erase the calendar and fill it in again asking in a grown-up voice, "What is today? What was yesterday? How many Fridays are in September?" They will use a pointer and point to numbers on the 100 chart or empty out and count the rocks that we are collecting for 100th day. Role playing teacher is playing with math and language.

We want students to become flexible and fluent in their use of math and academic language in both English and their home language. During learning-center time, we notice that a group of children who share the same home language might resort to this comfortable language while playing. However, if another child who speaks a different language joins them, the group switches back to their shared language of English. We do not discourage this behavior at all. We want the children to be fluent in both their home language and school language. This flexibility of language use is a useful and highly advanced skill.

Using Math Games to Support
Math Learning for ELLs

Math games are an integral part of our math learning. Games are "real world" to children. They are often even more real world than using money since not many young children have real-life practice using money. Games inherently include issues such as a need for accuracy and fairness when playing with a partner. Often teachers spend time at the beginning of the year soliciting ideas from their students for the routine of deciding who will go first in a game. The students can then use ideas from their list so a teacher does not have to intervene. This is a great way for children to incorporate ideas from many cultures.

The computer games are a wonderful way for children to learn. Two children at a time will learn to navigate through math programs together. The social language learned while solving problems on the computer together is as important as the math they are learning.

We use a large variety of games for math instruction, at learning centers, during math family nights, and for taking home to play with families. During math time, we take the time at the first of the year to learn game skills: rolling both number and dot cubes, flicking a spinner, moving a marker on a board, taking turns, and problem-solving during game playing. We model the game by playing it with a child as the class watches. Next all children play the games while we go from group to group to help. Later, during workstations at math time or during free-choice learning centers, the children are able to play the games without an adult.

Math Workshop: Routine and Structure

The math workshop structure is slightly different during small-group time than the reading and writing workshop. During this time, the children rotate to several workstations. Some stations are with an adult, and others are independent. This structure provides time for the teacher to be able to learn about each child's thinking. With the teacher, the children develop clear expectations for working independently, allowing the teacher to differentiate by working with small groups or individuals. (See Figure 7.3.)

Whole Group: Setting the Stage

The whole-group lesson begins at the meeting place on the floor, in a circle if there is room. First, there is a warm-up, a review, or an introduction to a new concept. As often as possible, teachers choose to start their teaching of

Figure 7.3 Kevan Miller's first graders have developed their class expectations for math workshop. They have used digital photos so that all students can understand.

a new concept by reading a book, which integrates math language and literacy and shows mathematics as communication. We often use Math Start books by Stuart Murphy, such as *Collecting Data* and *Matching*. After the book, we use manipulatives to model the new learning. The children join us in guided practice with their sets of manipulatives. This ten- or fifteen-minute opening time to introduce new learning or take a topic to a new level leads into workstations.

Small Groups: Guided Instruction and Practice

We prefer to group the children heterogeneously for workstations. A hetero-geneous grouping provides peer models for both math learning and language learning. There are times, however, when we group children homogenously, perhaps for reteaching or enriching. Regardless of how we choose to do this, the groups are flexible so that children have opportunities to work with dif-ferent children every day.

Small-group lessons make it possible to differentiate lessons for all stu-dents. In small working groups, there are more opportunities for talk, and it is also easier for the teacher to focus on each child. Small groups give the children time to practice skills, talk, and listen to others solve problems, and they also enable children to talk to the teacher and be responsible for their learning. Working with small groups gives the teacher time to adjust the lesson for each child in response to ongoing assessment. This ongoing assess-ing during small-group lessons in an informal setting is so much more valu-able than formal assessments.

During small-group time, station one is a teacher-directed group where the children and the teacher work together on problem-solving. For example, they talk through story problems with manipulatives and dry-erase boards. A child or teacher tells a story. Then each child chooses a way to solve the prob-lem, such as by using objects, drawing, acting out, using fingers, or looking for a pattern. Children share orally their problem-solving strategies.

Often the teacher fills in with words as ELLs point to their objects, use a quick sketch, or use their fingers. As the children pass through the stages of language acquisition, they will start adding language to their demonstrations. We might watch and say, "You made groups of ten and then took four away." This scaffolding is different for each child. The scaffolding will decrease as the child becomes more proficient in English and in this math concept. We will then transfer the focus of the scaffolding to a new level or to a new concept.

The scaffolding takes many forms: modeling, wait time, questioning, making conjectures, or providing the language for the child so he or she can solve the problem. When introduced to a new concept, even a child with English fluency will often revert to gestures until he or she is comfortable with the new vocabulary and may once again require a different level of scaf-folding. We ask questions even when we observe accuracy in a child's manip-ulation of tools. We want the child to understand and be able to explain why he or she was right in order to apply this thinking to other problems. Effective questioning along with careful observation help us understand a child's thoughts.

Let us look at two examples of scaffolding. Yesenia is not comfortable using the word *regrouping*, but she shows the teacher how she can trade ten ones for one ten. One of our math resource teachers, Jessica Sebag, offers support by giving her the words for what she is doing, "I see that you regrouped by trading your ten ones for one ten." Meanwhile, Hector may not have added *greatest* and *least* to his oral vocabulary, but they are part of his receptive language. When Hector gestures to the pile of rocks that has the greatest amount, Jessica says, "Yes, that pile of rocks is the greatest. Can you show us which pile has the least number of rocks?"

Story Problems
We assess the children daily as they work on a variety of word problems. Anecdotal notes from previous lessons make it possible to differentiate the same problem for each student. We find it extremely important to keep records of students with whom we worked. We also record which word problem we chose to make sure that we are giving opportunities for each child to have experience with a variety of structures and solution paths.

This variety in word-problem structures encourages the student to listen actively to the story problem. For example, "Josue had _____ pencils. He gave _____ to Ana. How many pencils does he have now?" Or "Josue had some pencils. He gave _____ to Ana. Now he has _____ pencils. How many pencils did Josue have to start with?"

Inserting numbers depending on the math needs of the child further differentiates the problem. If Malika and Haider are in the same group, the children can work with different numbers to solve the same problem about pencils. The numbers five and two are at Malika's instructional level, yet Haider's numbers are much higher. He can manage seventy-five and twenty-nine. Picking the right numbers for young mathematicians to use in a math problem is as important as choosing the right level of reading material for a young reader. To read more about using a variety of word structures and teaching children math problem-solving we suggest *Children's Mathematics, Cognitively Guided Instruction* by Carpenter, Fennema, Franke, Levi and Empson.

Small-Group Rotation and Independent Work

While station one is working with the teacher, stations two, three, and four are involved in independent or small-group math work. Students work with friends on activities such as attribute blocks, measuring, counting, familiar math games, computer games, rolling number cubes and adding, comparing numbers, estimating, open-ended math problems, looking at math books, or any math activities the children can do without assistance. Sometimes in these independent groups, children will use their home language. This is acceptable because a discussion using home language skills may result in a deeper understanding of the mathematical concept.

Some days the groups rotate every fifteen minutes so that all children go to all the workstations. In this type of rotation, the teacher works with every child in a small group each day. If a volunteer, an instructional assistant, or another teacher is in the room, there can be two teacher-directed stations.

If groups rotate after twenty minutes, the children go to two workstations in a day. The next day the children go to the other two workstations. Doing this rotation, the teacher meets with each child twice a week.

The last way we rotate is to go to a different station each day. The teacher meets with only one group a day but is able to have an extended time reteaching or enriching that group. By the end of the week, all students will have rotated through all stations. This last type of rotation works well in the first- and second-grade classrooms, where attention spans are longer and where children need to be involved in in-depth discovery learning or projects.

We use all three rotations depending on the math concepts, the maturity of the class, and the activities in which the children are involved. The key to success at these stations is that the tasks are interactive and that children know what to do at each station. Student confidence builds as children work together to understand math. Independent stations are always something that the children are comfortable doing without an adult present. Children have seen these activities modeled and have practiced them in a whole-group setting before tackling them in small independent groups. Talk is encouraged at all stations. If children are just practicing writing numbers, they can be practicing together on one large piece of paper with a friend.

Whole-Group Closure: Review and Self-Assessment

At the beginning of the year, we close our math time with self-assessment. We ask the whole group what went well. Then the whole group discusses ways to make math time a better learning experience for all. Later in the year, our usual closures involve math thinking. Students might share what they learned. The class could walk around to each station and listen as children explain what they accomplished or celebrate a student's math thinking. This opportunity for reflection on new learning helps students become metacognitive in their learning.

If we run out of time, we quickly put closure on the lesson by affirming something that we saw the students doing. Glancing at the clock, we might stand right where we are and exclaim, "The time slipped away today! It is time to go to music. However, I congratulate this group on their math thinking. I noticed that while they were working at their workstation they quickly solved their problem. When they finished solving their problem, they checked it by trying another way. That was good math thinking." Another way for quick closure is asking one child to share a strategy he or she used for solving a problem. For example, in September Mrs. Cordero's kindergarten students were visiting the math lab for the first time. Time was short for closure.

"Avash, can you tell everyone how you knew there were 23 students in your class?"

"I know 12 and 12 are 24. So 12 boys and 11 girls are 23."

"Thank you, Avash. The next time you come we will talk more about your strategy but now we have to wash our hands for lunch."

Questioning and Prompting During Math Workshop

To help children understand what they are learning and to help us assess their understanding, we ask questions or prompt students continuously. There are many levels of questioning. Students differ in understandings, and so they differ in the level of scaffolding they need to solve a problem. If a child is still not getting it, we know it is acceptable to change the numbers used in the problem so the child is able to use his or her strategies to solve the problem. If a child is still having difficulty after changing the numbers, we realize that the child may not be developmentally ready. This ongoing assessment is a natural part of learning in our classes and integral to our planning. The children do not see it as assessment but as being part of a learning community when they answer questions similar to these:

- What do you know? How did you solve that?
- What do you need to find out?
- What makes you think so?
- What can you use to help you? What else could you use? (Varieties of math tools are available for children to solve problems. We want them to be flexible in using them all: counters, hundreds boards, number lines, fingers, and so on).
- Can you do it another way? (We also want children to be flexible in using different strategies.)
- How did your partner figure it out?
- You seem stuck; what part is hard? Why?
- What are you going to do next?
- Can you show me another way to figure it out so you can check it to see if it is correct?
- How could you put this strategy down on paper? Could you draw a picture, write your numbers, or show how you used your fingers?

Children who are fluent English speakers are models for the other children as they answer. We pair children up or make small groups to solve problems. They listen to the other children answer the questions and soon pick up partial answers. Later they will be able to produce full explanations. With children who are in the silent stage of English acquisition, we give them the words. In Michelle Gale's room, this conversation took place when Yonathan was struggling with a problem. The question was, "Do you know how many new pencils we need to have?"

Michelle: What do you know?

Yonathan: [Silently looks down at his workspace.]

Michelle: Do you know how many pencils we have now?

Yonathan: [Looks at the cubes he has pulled from the basket: seventeen.]

Michelle: I see that you counted out seventeen cubes for our seventeen pencils. What else do you know?

Yonathan: [Silently shrugs his shoulders and looks around the room.]

Michelle: Do you know how many children are in the class?

Yonathan: [Nods head, stands, and counts children aloud.]

Michelle: That is smart math thinking. You knew you needed to know how many children were in the room so you counted the number of children. You even remembered to count yourself. What are you going to do next?

Yonathan: [Proudly counts out twenty-three cubes and lines them up parallel with the other seventeen cubes. Yonathan silently points to the extra cubes, counts, and sees that there are six more cubes in that row.]

Michelle: What do you know now?

Yonathan: Six pencils.

Michelle: You think that the class needs six more pencils for everyone to have a new one. Your partner did it another way. Hector, do you agree? Tell us about your thinking. Show us how you did it.

This expectation for talk and showing what you know during math starts on the first day. Children gradually acquire the math language they need and use it. We lessen the scaffolding as they gain confidence in using the language. When we introduce a new concept, we again have to feed the words to the children and provide more scaffolding. As we wait for the language to become accessible to each child, we model and accept drawings, acting out, pointing, and demonstrating with manipulatives as their thinking and solutions. It is important for children to justify their thinking and explain how they solve the problem.

Probing questions help guide the students' thinking. The goal is to get them to talk about their thinking independently as we gradually withdraw our support. The students' developing confidence prepares them to face new challenges. Just because a student is not fluent in English does not mean that we limit our questions to simple recall or lower-level ones. Students who are not yet fluent in English *can* answer higher-level questions. Therefore, we must ask the questions in context and use language they understand.

Modeling Silently

After saying we believe talk is essential for ELLs, Emelie must share a story about when she needed to use less talk. One year her first-grade class had nine children who had just come to America and were in the silent stage. Emelie was struggling trying to get them to learn a math concept. She does not remember what the concept was, but she does remember that it was 1:00 in the afternoon, after lunch and recess. She asked an expert from the district office to come in and observe her during the whole-group lesson time. She wanted suggestions. The specialist told her to try teaching it one time without any words and suggested that maybe the children were trying so hard to understand the English, the math language, and the math concept that it was just too much for them. She thought they might be tired from the day's onslaught of English.

The next day Emelie tried a similar lesson without using words. She fell silent after saying, "Eyes on me." Slowly with exaggerated movements, Emelie demonstrated the math with the manipulatives. The children watched her hands, carefully concentrating on the manipulation of the objects. The students' eyes lit up, and they grinned. They got it! From this experience, Emelie learned that modeling manipulatives in silence, at least once, when introducing a new concept could be helpful to ELLs. It was also a lesson in the great importance of physical materials and models for English language learners.

Planning and Designing Lessons That Meet a Wide Diversity of Needs

When planning for math workshop we ask these questions:

- What is the big idea, conceptually, that I want students to learn today?
- What from the previous lesson's assessments will help me in planning today's lesson?
- Will the children find today's math lesson purposeful, meaningful, and concrete?
- What provisions or visuals will help those with limited English understand?

- Is there a book that shows and tells about the math concept in a story format?
- What English does a child need to communicate or demonstrate his or her understanding?
- Are there ways for children at all stages of English acquisition to communicate or demonstrate their understanding?
- Which manipulative is best to teach this concept?
- What fresh manipulatives will best help reteach or practice the concept?
- What math language are the children learning today?
- What skills will the students need to control before attempting to play a game (for example, taking turns, rolling a number cube, using a spinner)?
- What language is essential for children to control in order to play a game (for example, "I rolled a four. I take four pennies.")?
- How can we build on the concept and differentiate the lesson through social interaction?
- Would total body movement or rhythm and songs enhance the lesson?
- Will there be a way to teach thinking?
- Will it be possible for children to solve the problems at different developmental levels?
- Will the lesson allow us to encourage and celebrate math thinking and flexibility in problem-solving?

Notice that we begin by reflecting on observations from the previous lessons. Planning from ongoing authentic assessment is essential for successful learning for ELLs because we have to start with what each child knows.

Similar to the observations of watching children seriate shapes with clay, we watch children make patterns or count objects or add bears to a balance scale to weigh an apple. As we watch a child draw pictures to solve a problem, we ask clarifying questions. Watching a child's body language is as important as listening to his or her oral responses. Through observations of work, play, and drawings, we assess the students. Through careful listening, prompting, and questioning, we try to negotiate meaning from their answers to see what level of math thinking they are at. Yes and no answers, nods of heads, short answers, a drawing, a gesture, or matching a set with a number card—these are all ways we can check for understanding.

After reflecting on our observations, we plan a new lesson based on what each child learned. This ongoing assessment helps us adjust lessons as we teach as well as plan the appropriate subsequent lesson that children need to continue in their understanding of the grade-level curriculum. The goal is always to make grade-level curriculum accessible and achievable for ELLs.

Placing Math Lessons in Context

For math lessons, we draw on the language, objects, and books of the current social studies or science unit of study. For example, in the fall, during the study of the cycle of the apple trees and the pumpkin vine, we use apples and pumpkins during math time. The children handle a variety of pumpkins and apples as they measure, weigh, count, sort, pattern, and graph. As they manipulate the red, yellow, and green apples and compare sizes and shapes of pumpkins, the children are learning math vocabulary that goes with math story problems: *less, more, equal, all together, how many left, ordinal numbers, sum,* and *difference.* It is, of course, enormously powerful to learn words like *pumpkins* and *apples* in a concrete and tactile fashion.

As the children go to an apple orchard, pick apples off a tree, and add them to their buckets, they acquire language that will help them in math. The students will then be able to follow simple math stories produced by their friends about picking and cooking apples. Because they have lived the language through this shared experience, many children will learn to produce their own simple math stories with help from adults. (See Figure 7.4.)

Figure 7.4 Uyen is learning both cooking and math vocabulary as she grates apples for pancakes.

During the study of the Pilgrims and Wampanoag, the children use nuts, corn, fish, and clamshells to count. They measure the size of the Mayflower and the longhouses. They subtract the number of people that died that first winter from the total that came over originally.

This constant integration of vocabulary from social studies, science, and language arts into the math curriculum makes math purposeful to students and gives them opportunities to develop and use their content vocabulary in a meaningful way. Assessments drive the instruction, and the vehicle used to deliver the lesson is content from the ongoing unit of study.

Planning for Language Acquisition

In planning math lessons, we think about the needs children have of acquiring so many types of language—academic language, concept and math language, social language, and language to label items. For example, primary children need to learn not only number sense, number concepts, and number theory, but also academic language, words such as *sort*, *pattern*, and *compare*. They need math and concept language, such as *more than*, *less than*, and *equal*, and they need social language to work with their friends. They need labeling language to identify math tools: *unifix cubes*, *number cubes*, *counters*, *balance*, *rulers*, *dry-erase boards*. When a lesson seems difficult for children, we ask ourselves, "Was it math concepts or language issues that made it difficult?" (See Figure 7.5.)

Learning About Problem-Solving and Application

Getting into problem-solving with ELLs can be a little tricky because you need them to understand what they are doing. One way we start is by solving the problems that are actually happening in our room. Emelie remembers that one year number-concept teaching and problem-solving started with pretzels. The daily schedule had the class eating lunch at 12:40. With such a long morning, she would pass out pretzels sometime in the midmorning. Counting out pretzels, or in other words, starting with what they knew, was the beginning of understanding number concept.

Some mornings each child had one big pretzel, another day, two twisty pretzels or three straight ones. Students learned that Emelie was going to satisfy their hunger, teach them to count, and teach them words about pretzels, all at the same time. Their problem-solving began when students noticed that children next to them received three pretzels and they had only one. They would quickly learn to hold up two fingers or say, "Two, please." That

ADAPTING STORY PROBLEMS FOR ELLS

The language of story problems can be adapted for English language learners by using plain sentence structures and vocabulary that students have as part of their receptive language. Simplified English story problems simplify the language, not the level of mathematics. Teachers can use more difficult Cognitively Guided Instruction (CGI) problem types, such as Join, Start Unknown problems, but use plain English to help the ELL understand the actions of the story problem. Someone with translation expertise can translate story problems into the students' primary language. This gives the teacher an opportunity to learn about students' mathematics learning and skills using their native language. Jessica Sebag, math resource teacher at Bailey's, adapted the following chart from Secada & Carey (1990). It provides some examples.

CGI Problem Type	English	Simplified English	Spanish
Join, Result Unknown	Mahnoor has 5 apples, and her friend, Tihare, gave her 6 more. How many apples does Mahnoor have now?	Mahnoor has 5 apples. Her friend gave her 6 more. How many does she have now?	Mahnoor tiene 5 manzanas, y su amiga, Tihare, le regaló 6 manzanas más. ¿Cuántas manzanas tiene ahora Mahnoor?
Join, Start Unknown	Rafael had some Yu-Gi-Oh! cards. He got 10 more cards and now he has 24 cards. How many Yu-Gi-Oh! cards did he start with?	Rafael has some (Yu-Gi-Oh!) cards. He got 10 more. Now, he has 24. How many did he start with?	Rafael tenía algunas tarjetas. Luego recibió 10 más y ahora, Rafael tiene 24 tarjetas. ¿Cuántos tarjetas tuvo Rafael al principio?
Compare, Difference Unknown	Katia has 6 pieces of candy, and Elena has 9 pieces of candy. How many more pieces of candy does Elena have then Katia?	Katia has 6 candies. Elena has 9 candies. Who has more? How many more?	Katia tiene 6 dulces, y Elena tiene 9 dulces. ¿Cuántos más dulces más tiene Elena que Katia?
Part-Part-Whole, Part Unknown	Armon has 15 books in all. Seven of his books are big and the rest are small. How many of Armon's books are small?	Armon has 15 books in all. Seven are big. The rest are small. How many are small?	Armon tiene un total de 15 libros. Siete de sus libros son grandes, y el resto son pequeños. ¿Cuántos de los libros son pequeños?

References
(a list originally from Round Rock Independent School District CGI Training, Round Rock, Texas)
Carpenter, T.P. & Moser, J.M. (1983). The acquisition of addition and subtraction concepts. In R. Lesh & M. Landau (Eds.), *The Acquisition of Mathematics Concepts and Processes* (pp.7–44). Orlando, FL: Academic Press.
Ghaleb, M. (1992). Performance and solution strategies of Arabic-speaking second graders in simple addition and subtraction word problems and relationship of performance to their degree of bilingualism. Unpublished doctoral dissertation, University of Wisconsin—Madison.
Secada, W. G. (1991). Degree of bilingualism and arithmetic problem solving in Hispanic first graders. *Elementary School Journal.* 92 (2), 211–229.
Secada, W.G. & Carey, D.A. (1990). Teaching mathematics with understanding to limited English proficient students (Urban Diversity Series No. 101, pp. 41–44). New York City: ERIC Clearinghouse on Urban Education, Institute on Urban and Minority Education. Teachers College, Columbia University. [Available through ERIC; also available as a PDF file at http://www.wcer.wisc.edu/ccvi/cgispider/articles/ AboutCGI.asp].

Figure 7.5 Adapting story problems.

year, Emelie realized that solving the dilemma of a late lunchtime with a snack of pretzels had launched math problem-solving. In addition, the students were on their way to understanding number concepts.

Learning to Comprehend, Tell, and Record Math Stories

As we teach basic math vocabulary, we start modeling math stories. We tell simple stories about what is happening in our lives at home or school. "When I was cooking dinner last night, the doorbell rang. It was my friend and her three children. What were we to do? We only had one pizza." We draw quick sketches of the story as we talk or take time to act the story out. Both ways help students comprehend.

Children soon want to tell their own "math happening" stories from their homes. To help the children, we listen for the math as they tell their stories. We tease the math story out and talk to them about math happening in their lives. If there is no math in it, we ask more questions. A student teacher, Lauren Nye, learned how to tease out a math story during this conversation with children at various stages of English language development.

Jonathan: One night my mom, brothers, and me were having supper.
Class: What happened next?
Jonathan: [mumbling] Nothing.
Juruvith: What did you eat?
Jonathan: Rice. [Everyone agrees rice is good.]
Sarah: How many brothers do you have?
Jonathan: Three.
Lauren: Jonathan, can you ask a math question to go with your story?
Jonathan: How many people at my house? [The class draws dots for three brothers, Jonathan, and his mother.]
Vincent: Five.
Jonathan: [grinning] I forgot, my Dad came.

Drawing a story while someone tells it helps all the learners see the story. Using props to represent the story also helps the learners understand. At the beginning of the year, some children will manipulate concrete objects such as apples. Next, we move to semiabstract with pictures of apples and finally to representation, where a manipulative such as a cube represents the apple. By the end of the year, the children are able to use counters to represent any object in their story. Of course, some children will jump past the concrete or move quickly from the concrete to the abstract. The use of concrete items and props at the beginning of the year or at the beginning of any new unit of study helps with vocabulary development and understanding of content and concepts. The children slowly start to mimic phrases they hear often in math story problems. They begin ending their stories with math questions.

How many _____ are there now?

How many _____ are left?

How many more _____ are there than _____?

Writing down children's math story problems and then using them to teach the whole class helps the children master story problems. They see their oral language written and understood by their peers. A group of two or three children at different levels of English ability prepares a story to tell, while the teacher acts as scribe. The children negotiate the story together, usually with relevant content language they all know, and then work on the details, the problem, and the question. They illustrate the problem and then present it to the class. Having a bank of contrived or real story problems to pull from with the children's names in them is powerful. It also helps the children see math in their everyday lives.

To help children understand math stories, we use other strategies. Teachers can clarify their talk by speaking in synonyms, using quick sketches or pantomime, or showing pictures or objects. For example, "Today we have some students absent. Look around to see who is not here today. How many chairs will we need at each table?" As I talk, I move to the chairs, pick one up and put it by Eliza's place and say, "A chair for Eliza and here is a chair for Edwin. How many more chairs do I need today?" The use of synonyms and prompts does not water down the language but helps clarify our meaning, just as using our body to pantomime helps clarify meaning for English language learners.

Using familiar content vocabulary during math stories provides a deeper understanding of what we are studying in science, social studies, or language arts. Using relevant content vocabulary helps the children concentrate on learning the academic language. The math stories become stories about Pilgrims searching for food to eat, animals and how many legs they have, or the plot and characters in a read-aloud. This reinforces vocabulary and gives the children hooks on which to attach their new learning. "The Wampanoag built three new canoes. They already had two. How many boats are in all?" These stories are fun for the children to dramatize. Children like to march through the forest and chop down trees to make boats. Watching the drama carefully, we can assess not only the math, but also the social studies understandings. We acknowledge and accept attempts. The attempts become more sophisticated as the children gradually learn to share real-life math stories and ask the appropriate math questions. This can take the whole year of practicing.

Children work through the math problems, joining, separating, or arranging objects into groups. As they become proficient in problem-solving, we help them to record their math stories by using symbols to make a math sentence. This again is more language to learn: *plus, minus, equal, more than, less than,* and *different than.* We are careful to read 4+2=6 in context. Four frogs were sitting on a log, and two more came to join them. Now there are six frogs sitting on the log. Many teachers use math journals so that children can explain their thinking through pictures and later symbols.

Learning About Number Concepts and Number Sense

For counting practice, teachers have many collections. The children select what they want to count. As they count toy airplanes, blocks, marbles, bugs, cars, crayons, rocks, or anything else we can find, we whisper, chant, sing, and shout the numbers and words. One button, two buttons, three buttons, four buttons, five buttons. The children choose things to count daily. We watch as children manipulate the counters and count, and we observe and prompt as the children learn to consistently move the counters or point to them and say the correct number.

As children learn to count orally, we make sure they practice matching the correct symbol to that number. We also make sure that children are able to write their oral numbers. If they count fourteen cars, they write the number. Interrupted counting is also very important for the children to become flexible in their ability to count and know what comes before and after a number. We will ask children to start at twenty-seven and count forward or start at seventy-nine and count backwards. Children must not just parrot numbers but must understand their counting. We look for meaningful counting as we check to see if the children are demonstrating one-to-one correspondence as they count. After a child masters counting by ones, he or she learns how to group objects by twos, fives, or tens. As the child masters any skill, we record it and use it as one piece of evidence to plan follow-up lessons for that child.

The children count together as a group, with a friend, or alone. Children are encouraged to speak aloud as they use their counters to demonstrate concepts such as one or two more or counting on and counting back, to solve addition and subtraction problems, and to describe positions with ordinal numbers. ELLs need to hear the numbers over and over.

Approximations are accepted and even celebrated. They are common for the teen numbers. It is hard for children to hear the difference in *seventeen* and *seventy* or *thirteen* and *thirty.* We simply enunciate the number for the child and repeat the numbers with an emphasis on the *teen*, "Yes, *thir-*

teen, four*teen,* fif*teen,* six*teen,* seven*teen.*" The other confusing part for second language learners is that all other two-digit numbers are written as they are spoken, for example, the number seventy-one; we say the tens first, then the ones. The teens are just the opposite. We say the ones first, then the tens. With time, the children will start to hear the ending sound and the order of the words and will be able to enunciate correctly.

Learning About Data Analysis

To teach the academic language, we model and clarify words as we work. "Today I will sort these shells before I count. Watch and help me as I put all the ones that look alike together. Can someone tell me a way to sort these? Is there another way? Eliza, how would you sort these? Now we have groups of shells that we sorted. First, count the shells in each group. Now compare the groups. How are the groups alike? How are the groups different? Can you graph them to make it easy for us to see?"

Many lessons like this using different objects give children practice with academic language while teaching them math language and skills. We watch to see if the children can sort. We make the lessons simpler or more challenging the next day according to our anecdotal notes. Eventually the children learn to sort, count, compare, and graph. They also develop an understanding of the academic words *sort, compare* and *graph.* They will learn to transfer these academic words and apply them during language arts, social studies, or science lessons.

Learning About Patterns

Primary-age children need to learn to recognize, copy, extend, create, and use patterns for problem-solving. As the children master simple repeated patterns and gradually proceed to complex repeated and growing patterns, they are also learning labeling vocabulary. Using interlocking cubes, links, or construction paper, children chant as they learn color words: Red, blue, red, blue, red, blue, red, blue. The meanings of concept words are internalized as they arrange their bodies to make a pattern of up, up, up, down, down, down or boy, girl, girl, boy, girl, girl, boy.

In small groups, the children paint, stamp, or color posters and charts that demonstrate patterning. Children label the patterns before displaying them on the wall. Because the children produce the visual with a group and so have ownership of it, they understand it and refer to it. Most often, the teacher does not make charts, posters, and other visuals before school but makes them with the whole class or with groups of children.

The children learn more vocabulary as we combine counting, patterns, and movement: jump three times, hop two times. Clap, clap, snap, snap. We learn to label shapes as we make patterns: Square, triangle, rhombus, square, triangle, rhombus. To learn to label money we make patterns: penny, nickel, dime, penny, nickel, dime. Children also make patterns without words by using music. They use triangles, rhythm sticks, and drums to make sound patterns.

This pattern work with words, objects, and movements will transfer into an "Aha" moment when a child sees the patterns in a hundred grid. The children start developing a deeper understanding of the base ten number system. Sometimes ELLs do not have the language to let us know that they have developed this understanding but will give us nonverbal clues. For example, when writing numbers one through one hundred on a hundred grid, they write the numbers top to bottom instead of left to right.

Learning About Geometry and Measurement

We continue to practice the vocabulary about shapes as we learn to draw self-portraits in art: Oval for our heads; rectangles for our legs and arms; square for our neck. We stick colored tape to the floor to make a triangle, rectangle, square, and large polygon. We refer to the shapes in conversation throughout the year.

"Everyone sit in the polygon, please, for our story."

"If you are wearing blue, line up at the rectangle."

"When you are finished, put your scissors in the triangle."

Teachers often use digital cameras. Mary Anne Buckley put pictures of her students in the hallway for us all to use as teaching tools. One display was of photographs of children standing next to objects, with labels such as, "Moises is taller than the bush and shorter than the tree." Another time she used children to illustrate position words. "Said is crawling through the pipe." "Yesmely is behind the tree." "Taminoor is third in line for the slide." Michelle Gale's class measured a very tall custodian, Wardell Mills, by drawing a line around his body on large paper. The class then used this drawing as they reenacted the book *How Big Is a Foot?* by Rolf Myller. (See Figure 7.6.)

Integrating the Arts into Math Lessons

Music, rhythms, drumming, choral reading, and chants help some children learn math. Weaving the arts through our lessons not only meets the needs of our kinesthetic learners, but also allows us to give alternative support to our ELLs. They will not have to rely only on language to comprehend a lesson.

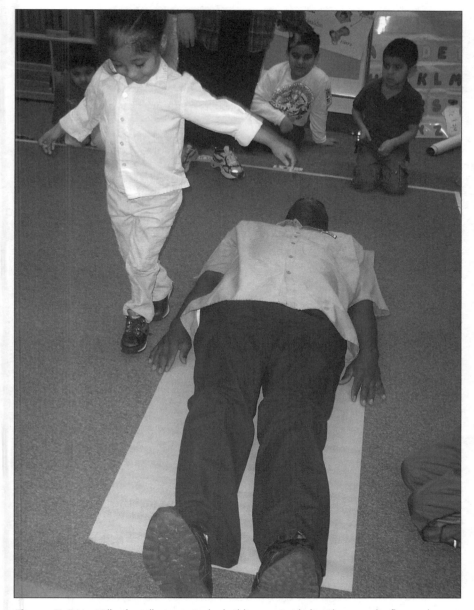

Figure 7.6 Mr. Mills, the tallest man in the building, patiently lies down on the floor to be measured by the class.

Art and movement help with the vocabulary of math, rote counting, memorizing of shapes, and the ability to see patterns all around us. Using their bodies to form shapes, numbers, and solids; to act out problems; and to position themselves takes abstract concepts and makes them concrete for the students. Using rhythm sticks to demonstrate the ability to create a pattern is easier for an ELL than demonstrating orally.

Singing puts the words into children's minds for repetition later on when they are at home. Rhythms are easy to recall when they are searching for "what comes next." When children are searching for that hard English word like *eleven*, *twelve*, or *fifteen*, they can refer to the rhythm or song to refresh their memory. Children often will make their first attempts at speaking English orally with whole-group chants. It is a safe way to speak.

Inviting Parents to Be Partners in Teaching Math

Several teachers invite parents into the classroom during the first twenty to thirty minutes of the day for Parents as Teachers time. About half of the mornings, the parents and children are engaged in math activities or games that the children play at the tables. The parent who spends time in the room in the morning is learning English, math language, and math concepts with his or her child, learning what the child is studying in school, and becoming familiar with the American school system. Often a family borrows a game to take home.

Parents are given number cubes and shown how they can use the cubes in their home language or in English to help their children recognize, name, add, and subtract numbers. Parents also learn how to play the card game More Than/Less Than (also known as War or Top-It). The children love to play this with their parents.

As the parents play the games, their confidence in understanding and speaking English grows. Many of our parents had little schooling in their home countries. They are enthralled with the pattern blocks and will sit and make patterns next to their children or help them combine cubes to make patterns. We hope that becoming aware of patterns together with their children will carry over into their homes.

We also teach games to families at family math nights designed for the whole school or for a grade level. The families leave with the games in their hands to play at home. The families sit at round tables learning to play games applicable for all developmental levels. Sometimes we go into the gym for physical activities like the one shown in Figure 7.7. The adults leave with a better understanding of the way their children receive math instruction and with ways to support their children at home. We have translators at these family math nights to help parents understand the instruction.

In conclusion, the following list summarizes the many ways teachers can help ELLs acquire the math concepts, math language, and thinking skills needed to succeed.

Figure 7.7 Mariana and her mother were quick to form a triangle with their bodies at family math night, while other families experimented with their own geometric shapes.

- Actively engage children in mathematical communication through discussion, reading, writing, and listening to mathematical ideas.
- Design lessons and learning activities that provide for visual support and concrete learning.
- Design lessons where talk and practice are encouraged.
- Differentiate the instruction according to each child's need.
- Design and make posters, charts, and visuals with the children to display in the room.
- Teach children to verbalize their thinking.
- Assess understanding in many ways other than pencil-and-paper tasks.
- Accept attempts and approximations.
- Look for good math thinking and intelligence in errors as well as in correct answers.
- Teach math all day based on ongoing assessment and as opportunities arise.
- Use games to reinforce the learning.
- Involve parents in math learning.
- Teach mathematical concepts in meaningful contexts.

SCIENCE WORKSHOP

Science activities provide numerous and varied opportunities for language development. The language of science is naturally embedded in science activities, including teacher demonstrations and student experiments. When students are discussing their observations, reasoning through a problem, or stating conclusions, they need to use language that is precise, objective, and scientifically accurate.

Anna Uhl Chamot and J. Michael O'Malley, *The CALLA Handbook*

The first graders had discussed their way through *Bob the Snowman* by Sylvia Loretan and Jan Lenica. As Tess read it numerous times, the children had acted out shivering, sweating, melting, and evaporating. They had watched their wet handprints disappear from the chalkboard. They had watched the steam from the boiling teapot condense on the cookie sheet Tess held above the spout.

Tess was repeating, "wet, wet" to José as she touched his wet hand to his cheek. Max and Elliot were hatching a scheme to create a full-blown cloud in the classroom. Stephanie, in her own little world, was quietly huffing into the air, trying to see her breath. Edwin, watching his handprint fade on the board, pulled his hand inside his sweater sleeve. Waving it around like an elephant's trunk, he cried, "My hand's gone. My hand's gone." No one seemed particularly interested, so he prepared to step up his efforts.

Tess quickly drew what was happening to the water drops in a cloud in order to refocus Edwin. There was a moment of revelation when Edwin proclaimed, "They're doing the round thing! It's like a circle. It's a . . . a . . . a cycle."

Tess asked the class, "What kind of cycle is it?" Franklin thought and then said, "A snow cycle." Vivian risked her first input to the discussion and quietly said, "Maybe water cycle?"

Edwin, beside himself with excitement, announced triumphantly, "There more is water cycle! The air—it's the rain, it come down and it wets all the flowers then it . . . the steam goes up and it makes a cloud then it comes down again!" Max nodded sagely. "It goes around and around a billion times!" he agreed.

Just as in other workshops, the ELLs in Tess's classroom needed the support of peers and teachers during science time. Let's listen in on another conversation, this one in Emelie's class, at the beginning of science time. The class was talking about things they might see at the petting zoo the next week.

Ashley: I went to North Carolina and they had a . . . . I don't know what it is in English.

Emelie: You can say it in Spanish.

[Long wait time.]

Classmates: Was it something you eat, or something to play with?

Ashley: No it was something you put the eggs in. And then, when, then . . .

[Again she ran out of words but used her hands to help us understand.]

Emelie: Cracking open? Was it an egg cracking open? Did they call it an incubator?

Classmates: Was it a duck? A chicken?

Emelie: Were they in something to keep the eggs warm?

Ashley: Yes! Yes!

Emelie: The thing they put it in is an incubator. The incubator keeps the eggs warm until they hatch. You saw them hatch. The eggs cracked open and came out. Let's all say that long word . . . in cu bat or. Incubator.

Class: Incubator.

Classmate: Was it white or brown eggs?

Ashley: White. It tried to bite me but it didn't.

Ashley proudly points to her wrist and smiles. She is happy that with our support she was able to tell her story and that we understood it.

In this chapter we will focus on strategies and techniques that help all children learn scientific concepts. As with other subjects, science is taught throughout the day as well as during science workshop, and we teach the rich content using techniques that make it accessible to all learners. Teachers support the development of scientific language and content by

- Designing a place for hands-on science learning.
- Making daily reading of nonfiction books a priority.
- Teaching children how to select and read a variety of science books.
- Changing books in the classroom often.
- Teaching children how to record data, label diagrams, draw and write nonfiction.
- Planning long-term units based on curriculum objectives.
- Planning whole-group and small-group learning experiences to include all learning styles, abilities, and levels of English.
- Teaching children how to ask questions and search for answers through inquiry.
- Teaching mini-lessons across the curriculum that support scientific learning.
- Using a variety of alternative assessments and performance assessments.
- Reflecting on assessments, then reteaching and enriching.
- Enhancing science learning through field trips, gardens, murals, technology, student-generated museums, and neighborhood walks.
- Involving parents creatively.

We are always aware that it is more than science language we are responsible for teaching. The children must learn the necessary academic language that goes hand in hand with science, such as *predict, investigate, research, discover,* and *conclude.*

Designing a Physical Space for Learning

Children flourish in a science workshop setting where they can receive the support and scaffolding they need as they eagerly add both information and

Figure 8.1 Ada Prabhavat's classroom science center is ever changing.

processes to their scientific knowledge. The core of science workshop is books, visual images, and lots and lots of "stuff" for children to put their hands on such as sticks, rocks, leaves, bugs, beakers, magnets, water, sand, plants, worms, and so on. (See Figure 8.1.) As students work together to arrange, categorize, and investigate these kinds of items, they will become comfortable with the language of science.

The classroom has a special place for nonfiction books where the children browse and learn from photographs, illustrations, and diagrams in a variety of picture books that are essential for science learning. Books displayed with their covers out invite young learners to open them. During buddy reading, before school, or during choice time, children pore over the books, chatting about the pictures. Students are adept at reading information from pictures or reading science books. Children receive mini-lessons that provide instruction and guided practice on how to acquire knowledge from pictures, diagrams, graphs, and other graphic organizers. Many times, we find a book stashed under a cupboard or behind a bookcase, where children selfishly hide their favorite ones from each other.

We gather as many books as possible on the same subject from the school library for our units of study. We know we will need the books to help with vocabulary as well as with concepts as we teach the lessons. These books are stored in a basket labeled appropriately. When writing or choosing books for reading time, children borrow from and return books into the designated basket. They revisit the same book often to copy words or find information from a picture.

Sometimes we take several children with us to the school library to help select new books to check out for our class library. This small-group mini-lesson is an opportunity to teach the children where to find their favorite sections, such as dinosaurs, animals, or volcanoes. Our students may go to the library daily to check out a book in English or in their home language. The nonfiction books lure the children into reading with their vibrant pictures. ELLs learn a great deal of science information and concepts as they take these picture books home to discuss them with their families in their home language.

As units change, new books related to the subject are on display in the science center. We also use images and sounds from the computer by making slide shows, using CD-Roms, online video streaming sites, and computer software. Often the software is bilingual. We give the children time to use these programs in both languages.

Children often gather around the science table to touch, smell, taste, and observe displayed artifacts. For example, there may be an ant farm with related posters and books. As children observe, they make sketches in the lab book. Tools the children need to be scientists are available: magnifying glasses, microscopes, lab books, beakers, markers, and so on.

We leave out science centers, data gathering charts, and journals all year. Our science resource teacher, Lynn Riggs, has helped us realize that there is value in observing over time. Taking temperatures or measuring shadows or plant growth give children lots of practice with measurement tools and with the language for the tasks. Patterns and cycles are revealed only through analysis of cumulative data, thus the children need to gather data over days, weeks, and months. We often ask parents to come into the class in the morning to help with daily weather/flora/fauna data. It relieves us from doing it every day and gives the parents an opportunity to learn side by side with their children.

We encourage children to bring in found objects for the science/nature center. Children add fossils, seed pods, and insects found at recess to the table. At the end of the year, Jennifer sneaked an egg out of her refrigerator. In the science center, she made a nest of cotton balls and tissue and expectantly placed it in the window waiting for the chicken to hatch. After deciding the air conditioning was making the room too cold, Jennifer wanted to take it out to recess so it would hatch in the hot June sun. Even a trip to the science lab to talk with Lynn Riggs did not discourage her from insisting that the egg would hatch. Sadly, the egg cracked at the end of the day when she was putting it into her backpack. To learn more about eggs hatching, Xavier and Thomas read her the book *Egg to Chick* by Millicent E. Selsam the next morning.

Children jot down "I wonder" questions—questions they want to explore further—and discoveries in the science center "I wonder" book.

Teachers use questions such as "I wonder why Jennifer's egg didn't hatch?" for planning lessons or for children to use in their individual inquiry learning. Small groups go the science lab during free-choice learning to work on their inquiry ("I wonder") questions with the science resource teacher.

Typical discovery entries found in a class log are:

- While looking at a bird's nest, Trini said, "I tried to use the magnifying glass to look at things. I think it's made of hair."
- Zayd remarked during water exploration, "The water weighed 100 on both sides. What are the bubbles? Are they like what comes out of fish mouths?"
- During a gas, liquid, solid balloon experiment, Haider wrote, "I squeeze the liquid balloon. The water moves."

Meeting a Diversity of Needs Through Long-term Planning

As mentioned in the social studies chapter, our faculty has been studying and learning how to design long-term lesson plans using Grant Wiggins's and Jay McTighe's Backward Design method. Using this method for science learning as well, we plan together as a team, deciding on the essential questions we wish to consider during a unit of study. We use the curriculum to determine the skills and knowledge that children need to master. Then we develop alternative assessments for the units. Lastly, we decide on activities that will most efficiently help the learners.

Several units our teams have written are on science topics teachers across the county are required to teach: water cycle, plants\life cycles, seasonal changes, and change over time. Our units are continuously evolving. We change things that do not work and are constantly revising the questions to make them ELL-friendly. There are also visual or performing arts objectives taught and integrated throughout the units.

Teachers use the unit plans for designing mini-lessons in reading, writing, and math workshops as well as in science workshop. In math, the students learn about measuring while estimating the weight and circumference of pumpkins and apples using standard and nonstandard measurement. During reading/writing workshops we teach mini-lessons on such topics as nonfiction writing and how to use the table of contents and index to search for information.

Teams write rubrics for the assessments that involve movement, murals, drawings, writing, or oral presentations. There are no assessments requiring only written answers since that would prevent many of our ELLs from demonstrating their learning. These rubrics assess learning in science as well as in visual or performing arts.

The following is a unit plan with both art and science objectives created using the Backward Design method of planning.

STAGE 1—DESIRED RESULTS

Established Goals
- Established Goal(s) Seasonal Changes over time, plant/life cycle.
- SOL Life Processes K.6: Describe some simple changes animals and plants undergo during life cycle.
- SOL Life Processes K.6: Describe how plants change as they grow.
- SOL Life Processes K.6: Students will investigate and understand basic needs and life processes of plants and animals.
- SOL Scientific Investigation, Reasoning and Logic K.2: Students will investigate and understand that humans have senses that allow one to seek, find, take in, and react or respond to information in order to learn about one's surroundings.
- SOL Earth Patterns, Cycles and Change K.8: The student will investigate and understand simple patterns in his/her daily life. Key concepts include weather observations; the shapes and forms of many common natural objects including seeds, cones, and leaves; animal and plant growth.
- Kennedy Center Art Standard One: Identify and demonstrate movement elements and skills in performing dance.
* Kennedy Center Art Standard Seven: Make connections between movement and other disciplines.

Understandings
- Multiple resources and our five senses help us learn about a topic.
- Plant cycles have events that repeat in a particular sequence.
- Each step of the plant cycle represents changes from the previous step.
- Certain conditions can change a life cycle.
- Living things have basic needs for survival.
- Living things and our world change with the seasons.
- Temperature affects weather and seasonal changes.
- Art is a tool for expressing what you see and feel.
- Dance is a language of body, energy, space, and time

Students will know . . .
- Sequence of seed to fruit.
- Vocabulary of plant cycle.
- Basic needs of a plant.
- People's role in plant growth.
- We can observe changes using our five senses.
- People adapt to changing seasons.
- Elements of dance (body, space, time, and energy).

Essential Questions
- How do you learn about a topic?
- What is a cycle?
- How do animals change through the seasons?
- How do plants change through the seasons?
- How do living things change?
- What makes each season different?
- How can we use our five senses to observe changes in our environment?
- How do people change through the seasons?
- How can you show the plant cycle with your body?
- How can you show the plant cycle with your drawing?

Students will be able to . . .
- Read thermometers and graph weather changes over time.
- Infer from observations and make predictions about plant cycle.
- Describe plant cycle orally, pictorially, through movement, and/or in writing.
- Identify characteristics of living things and how they adapt to different seasons.
- Use elements of dance to act out vocabulary in motion and create a movement phrase.

171

STAGE 2—ASSESSMENT EVIDENCE

Performance Tasks

Students will create a four-part pictorial representation of the seasons incorporating the elements they know change in each picture. Two parts will be completed in Fall, and two parts will be completed in Spring. Representations will show that students recognize change in living things—animals, humans, and plants—over time. Final products will be arranged by the children to show the cyclical nature of the seasons. Children will present their representations to the class.

Other Evidence

- Interview in both fall and spring: tell me the story of seasons, apple tree cycle, pumpkin cycle.
- Anecdotal records.
- Entries in learning logs.
- Movement—interpretive dance to music like Vivaldi's 4 Seasons—to show plant cycle from seed to fruit and to act out vocabulary.
- Records of experiments and science journals.
- Data displays (weather graphs, plant-cycle growth chart).
- Revisions to Venn diagrams and other graphic organizers.
- Drawings/paintings with oral comments.
- Reflections using photographs.

STAGE 3—LEARNING PLAN

- Identify and describe plant/life/season cycles.
- Hook students in on essential questions, plant experiments, nature walks, field trip to apple orchard.
- Equip students with read-alouds where students learn to use hand signals for I understand or I don't understand.
- Use think-and-draw activities after read-alouds to see students' understanding of concepts.
- Give movement lessons on how to dance and use elements of dance to put vocabulary into motion.
- Use data displays to show comprehension—weather graphs, plant experiment growth charts.
- Revise/rethink with children through concept maps, schema charts, movement, and role playing.
- Evaluate students through interviews, conversations, movement, and art.
- Tailor lessons to children by working in small groups using a variety of resources, realia, and requiring all students to draw/orally tell story/move to show comprehension of basic understandings.
- Organize mini-lessons based on anecdotal notes, interviews, drawings, and movement.

Key Activities

- Use TIC (think, investigate, conclude) graphic organizer to find out what do you think about cycles, how can we investigate, and what do we conclude?
- Once a week go for nature walk, take photos, and reflect with a discussion about how we used our five senses to learn about our environment.
- Hands-on Exploration: sort and plant seeds; collect, sort, and graph leaves; conduct experiments with seeds, stems, leaves, roots, and flowers.
- Collect and graph data over time using temperature and weather.
- Teach elements of dance through mini-lessons to demonstrate vocabulary and show sequence of cycles.

- Teach observational drawing.
- Make connections using read-alouds and discussions to what is a cycle and other life cycles in their lives.
- Use shared reading and small-group read-alouds to help children think about their thinking and learn to ask questions.
- Create anchor charts after read-alouds to show students' understanding of text and how their schema is changing over time.
- Use mini-lessons in writing workshop on using charts to write nonfiction, labeling, writing sequence, and referring to nonfiction books for information.
- Use nonfiction books to model mini-lessons and think-alouds about important concepts:
  1. Study of leaves—shapes and colors of leaves.
  2. Study of seeds—shapes and colors of seeds.
  3. Study of flowers—shapes and colors of flowers.
  4. Study of seasons—patterns of weather and temperature.
  5. Study of life cycles—patterns of plant/animal/season cycles.
  6. Study of animals—basic needs of water, food, shelter, and clothing/fur.

RUBRIC				
Trait	*Early Emergent*	*Developing Emergent*	*Emergent*	*Novice*
Listening/ Speaking	Rarely uses terminology to express ideas.	Sometimes uses terminology to express ideas.	Frequently uses terminology to express ideas.	Always uses terminology to express ideas.
Cycles	Misunderstanding of steps in a cycle.	Partial understanding of steps in a cycle.	Substantial understanding of steps in a cycle.	Thorough and complete understanding of steps in a cycle.
Nonfiction Drawing/ Writing	Major inaccuracies in presentation of information.	Some inaccuracies in presentation of information.	Generally accurate in presentation of information.	Completely accurate in presentation of information.
Movement	Ineffective in demonstrating movement.	Somewhat effective in demonstrating movement.	Generally effective in demonstrating movement.	Highly effective in demonstrating movement.

Science Workshop: Routine and Structure

Students are familiar with the routine of workshops: a whole-group lesson that is followed by small-group or individual work and ends with a meeting of the whole group to provide closure. This same routine is used for science workshop.

Whole Group: Setting the Stage

At the beginning of a new unit of study, the class often makes a chart together entitled: Our schema about _____. We accept what the children think they know. Even if the information is incorrect, we write it down. These misconceptions help us plan what we need to emphasize in our teaching as we investigate the topic.

In the September 2004 *Science and Children*, David T. Crowther and John Cannon wrote about changing KWL to THC for science purposes. Crowther and Cannon changed the "What do I **K**now? What do I **W**ant to learn? What did I **L**earn?" to "What do you **T**hink? **H**ow can we find out? And what do we **C**onclude?" These changes, according to Crowther and Cannon, "offer a framework that prepares children to think scientifically, relates to the nature of science, and integrates more purposeful communication by children." Our science resource teacher, Lynn Riggs, has tweaked it just a little to say: "What do you **T**hink? How can we **I**nvestigate? And What do we **C**onclude?" And so the schema chart that we write and adjust is TIC.

To activate prior knowledge and process new information we start subsequent whole-group lessons in a variety of ways. We talk as we observe artifacts, go on a nature walk, compile "I wonder" questions about a poster, observe insects scurrying in a box, or read a Big Book together. Because we use library books and trade books as our science texts, we read aloud many books during the unit.

Kevan Miller's first-grade class provides a good example of a whole-group lesson. They are on their second day of a series of "What could live here?" lessons. Notice both the analytical thinking Kevan is modeling and how she is always scaffolding for her students. Along with the fact that scientists are analytical thinkers, Kevan is also teaching the children to make observations and modify their thinking as they acquire more information.

Kevan had brought in a glass tank that contained a layer of coarse sand. The children had brainstormed their ideas, and each had predicted what could live in the tank by drawing in their science journal. On this day Kevan has brought in a pile of animal books that she places on the floor next to her. The children sit down with her in a circle, with the tank in the middle. Kevan has two empty baskets, one marked *Yes* and one marked *No*. Kevan holds up a book about turtles and asks the children if they could live in the tank. The children tell her to put it in the Yes basket. They continue to separate the pile of books into the baskets. This is all so visual that even Christine, a Vietnamese student who speaks only the most basic survival English, is able to join in the decision-making.

The following day Kevan writes a clue on large chart paper clipped to her Big Books stand that says, "It is smaller than a kitten. It is bigger than a spider." There is a short discussion among the group, with much gesturing, to decide what size would accurately match the clue. Kevan has pictures of a kitten and a spider at hand, in case Christine needs this extra level of scaffolding to help her understand the vocabulary or the size concept, but she seems to be getting the idea from everyone's gestures.

Now that the children have agreed on a general size, Kevan pulls out the Yes basket of books, and the children go through the process of elimination again based on the more specific size information. The No basket is filling up, and there are only a few books left in the Yes basket. The anticipation and the level of curiosity are building. Christine, Ronal, and Karol have been engaged in each step of the process because Kevan has provided such visual support.

It is science time on Friday afternoon, and Kevan writes another clue on the chart paper. "It does not have fur. It does not have feathers." She sketches a quick illustration so she can point as she says the words "fur" and "feathers," because she is anticipating that Christine and Ronal will need help with this vocabulary

Kevan is holding up a turtle book and a frog book. She points to the pictures on the front of the book as she asks Ronal, "Would a turtle live here, or is it going to be a frog?" Ronal shakes his head to both. Kevan is not sure now whether he understands or not. Kevan looks at Christine and asks, "Christine, could you help me with this?" Christine shakes her head.

Gavin, an English speaker, asks, "Do you have any more clues for us?"

Kevan responds, "I do. I have one more clue for you. This is your last clue for today."

She starts writing, "It has a shell." She draws some examples; a snail shell, a turtle shell, a scallop shell, and a crab shell.

Kevan asks the class, "Now, what are we looking for?" She holds up a book from the Yes basket and, passing it to Gavin, says, "Gavin would you check this book for animals with shells?"

Ronal says, "This basket is winning," as he points to the No basket. The children want to count the books. They have seventeen in the No basket and six in the Yes basket.

Kevan announces, "You are going to have time to make another prediction in your science journals. You need to decide what I'm going to bring in next week to live in here." She picks up some of the books and says, "Am I going to bring in a turtle or a snail or a hermit crab or maybe another kind of crab?" Kevan drops her voice to a whisper, puts one hand to her head, and wrinkles her forehead to indicate she is thinking hard. "What do you think? Just think in your head, 'What can it be?'"

"Abha, do you have an idea?" Kevan tells her to get her science journal. Kevan shows the class how Abha is going to turn to the next clean page, and off she goes. Kevan asks three more children who have ideas to bring up their journals. She models less specifically each time how to find the right page, and then she sends everyone off to draw with the group at their worktables.

Kevan moves from student to student, drawing each one into conversation about their predictions, feeding them the vocabulary if they need it, and asking questions to try to get them to use the unfamiliar words in their responses.

Christine draws a hermit crab. She has been nodding often during today's discussion, and Kevan thinks the girl understands, but then she starts to draw a dog. Kevan wonders if she thinks there will be one animal with a shell and one with fur? Kevan is not sure what Christine is thinking so she pulls out some shells to show her. Christine draws another hermit crab. On Monday, the class is thrilled to see that their tank contains two hermit crabs!

Small Groups: Engaging Children

After dismissing children from whole group, Kevan used the workshop time to go from group to group to give support where needed. The children also had time to explore on their own or chat with others in their work group about their predictions. This guided practice time is essential for learning.

Often these small groups are working on an experiment, such as testing different types of soil for a worm's habitat. Working in small groups encourages children who might not participate in a whole group. Each member of the small group will have a vital part to play if the experiment is to be successful.

For example, a small group searching through magazines for animals will need everyone in the group to complete the task of cutting, sorting, and gluing animals in their correct habitats. To encourage conversations, children do not make individual booklets of their findings but glue the animals on one of several colorful large papers draped across tables and on the floor. Children will have to work together to communicate in a variety of ways as they fill up the long blue paper with animals that live in water, or the long beige paper with animals that live in the desert.

A teacher roaming around the room will assist and probe where necessary, but children will work out on their own how to work together. This also gives children who speak the same language time to share their learning.

The following conversation among four boys with various degrees of English acquisition illustrates learning during their small-group investigation. The voices of Bruce Lee, Gabriel, Vincent, and Erick tumble over each other in their excitement as they explore magnets.

"The stick [bar magnet] is sticking to things on two sides. It's not sticking inside so it pushes out. The stick doesn't come out, it sticks inside the other magnets. Does the *N* mean not stick and *S* mean stick? The ball goes up and sticks. The balls are stick to the small sticks. The ball magnet is weak; the curvy [horseshoe] magnet is strong. A little strong for little hands. Hey, it pushes, then turns to stick. No stick. Stick. I stick the ball on one side and it swing around to the other side. It spins. I know the *N* and *S*. It's in the book. It is north and south." This discussion goes on until a very loud shout goes up from the group. Gabriel has discovered that if you put a rod magnet inside a hollow cylinder magnet a certain way, it will shoot across the room. We decide it is time for whole-group closure!

Whole-Group Closure: Opportunities for Review and Assessment

The routine is the same as in other workshop settings. The class gathers on the floor in the meeting area to summarize and review their investigations. Students add or change information on their schema charts. Often children find that their prior knowledge was inaccurate. For example, on the TIC chart about apples, a kindergarten student said, "If you plant an apple seed, a flower comes up." Mrs. Gale entered that information. Later on in the unit the class added more information to show that apple seeds grow sprouts, then an apple tree, then pink blossoms, and, finally, apples.

Children share their projects or journal entries with the class as another way of reflecting and bringing closure to the workshop. Children's entries are often in the form of labeled diagrams and illustrations, with words from schema charts, books, or posters as labels. The class adds to webs or other types of graphic organizers, using both pictures and words so that children can refer to them as needed.

When we study such things as the life cycle of plants, the water cycle, and magnets, closure review often takes the form of whole-group or small-group movement activities. After deciding which performance mode would work best, children create and add new movements to represent their new understandings. It is fascinating to watch the little bodies form shapes and use movement to explain these new insights into the unit of study.

We have showcases in the hallways, and often children place projects or findings in them or on tables, creating mini museums in progress. During closure time, as a way of review, the class can decide what should go in the hallway and what labels they need to write to let other classes know what they are learning.

Storytelling: An Opportunity for Learning and Assessment

Pretending to be a bird in the rain forest, a saguaro in the desert, a wild animal of the savannah, or a frog from the woodland is a way to make storytelling an integral part of teaching, learning, and assessing during a science unit of study. For example, a teacher could teach a lesson pretending to be a saguaro. Likewise, children could work together to research the habitat of a desert through books and computer programs. Then a group of students could tell the story from "behind the mask of the saguaro," telling what they know from the saguaro's point of view. "I am a saguaro. I live in the desert. I can grow to be thirty feet tall. My flowers bloom at night. A woodpecker pecks a hole in my arms. Native Americans used to eat my fruit." This could be written and/or oral. It could stand alone or be part of a tableau on the desert habitat. It could be part of a dance, part of a drama set to music, or part of a presentation on deserts. With art as a mask, it is often easier for the child to talk because the child feels as though the tree or the animal is talking.

Drawing and Movement: Alternative Ways to Assess Knowledge

Ongoing assessment drives the daily science workshop lessons. Children are encouraged to draw their understandings with journal entries. We listen carefully to discussions. In addition, we have found that assessing movement during science is beneficial. It is often difficult for children to explain concepts and information in their own words. Through movement, however, they are able to show their learning.

Two examples of using movement to teach as well as assess occur during the water-cycle and magnet units. A description of some of the science experiences during these units will help explain how movement leads to deeper levels of understanding of concepts and vocabulary for the students as well as informs teachers of confusions, inaccuracies, or gaps in their learning.

Because we wait for cold weather to teach the water cycle, children are able to put cups of water outside to freeze overnight. They then bring them in and watch the ice melt. They are surprised to see the water evaporate over a period of days and are amazed at what happens when a sauce pan of snow melts, starts to boil, and disappears during an experiment. Their eyes widen

Figure 8.2 Iliass, Catie, and Vinh demonstrate their understanding of evaporation in the water cycle through movement.

as a tissue placed over the steam is saturated. They carry cups out to catch snow and do the same experiment over again, placing their cups where they think snow will melt quickly or slowly. During closure time, the teacher narrates as children use their bodies to review the latest discoveries. Teachers watch for understandings or confusions.

For example, when a child is moving fast and running around in circles, we know that he or she doesn't quite get evaporation. However, when we see Trini slowly rising from her imaginary puddle with her arms reaching to the sky, we know she understands that the water becomes gas. We stop and ask the children who understand it to demonstrate their interpretation for the rest of the class. Then we ask those children to explain to everyone why they are moving slowly and why they are slowly lifting their arms skyward. (See Figure 8.2.)

Figure 8.3 In his science journal, Nestor describes the importance of water through drawings and words.

At recess, Emelie's students observed the snow on the blacktop as it turned to water and then evaporated over a period of a few days. Students drew a chalk ring around a mound of snow to measure the evaporation. One day as the students lined up to come in after recess, Bruce Lee noticed the melted snow had disappeared. He began an impromptu dance shouting and waving his arms to the sky, "It evaporated. It's gas!" Emelie made a mental note of this assessment of Bruce Lee's understanding of both science vocabulary and the water cycle.

Bailey's has a courtyard with a small pond, which students check daily to see if it is frozen. Children go outside, take and record the temperature, and learn from daily observations over time. We read books that show the ice crystals and water droplets sticking together in the clouds. We learn how to draw and label clouds with ice crystals attaching to water droplets getting heavier and snowflakes falling. Diagrams are drawn and redrawn with arrows and labels. Children learn how to read and write graphic information. (See Figure 8.3.) We continue to make additions or adjustments to performances that represent new information.

Children move their bodies to represent these hands-on experiences and vocabulary. "Show me how ice crystals and water droplets would stick together." "You are a puddle of melted snow; you are liquid, now you are evaporating slowly, slowly, slowly. Now you are going up, up, up as gas. Show me with your body how it evaporates." Carefully, one part at a time, the teacher talks through the cycle using the correct scientific vocabulary.

Students are also learning dance and movement skills such as using space, levels, timing, energy, and positioning as they interpret their learning in new ways.

Movement allows ongoing assessment to lead to immediate reteaching of any areas of confusion. It is easy to see the issue blocking a child's understanding. The class can stop and watch another child's movement to understand a concept, or we can refer to a book or a drawing. Then we can move forward, adding more information through movement to our dance. This ongoing assessment drives the planning as to what experiment to teach next or what part of the cycle to review, and it includes looking to see if the students understand movement skills. The children may be ready for a new skill such as becoming snowflakes moving around a space without touching each other.

When the children are ready, they use dance, a variety of movements, or tableaux to tell the entire water cycle. Children are familiar enough now with the language of the unit to take turns being the narrator. Adding music helps slow down bodies and set the mood. This final performance is an assessment. Teachers use the rubrics to assess both science and movement learning.

After a few times through the movement piece, the desire for an audience arises. We might troop next door to another class or quickly write a note inviting a class to pop in on their way back from PE. This year three children added narration and background music to a four-minute video recording of our dance with the help of Jon Leavitt in the communications lab. The fifth grade used the video for schoolwide viewing on the Bailey's news program. The video went home every night in a child's backpack to a different family, enabling the parents to learn what we were studying as well as the English words for the water cycle.

During the study of magnets, the children were to learn the following vocabulary: *magnetic field, force, energy, pull, push, repel, attract, north,* and *south.* They explored a variety of types of magnets and found out what these words meant through multiple experiments at small-group time.

When it was closure time, the children had lots of fun pairing off and using movement to demonstrate magnets attracting, pulling, or pushing. They created ways to show the magnetic field.

Because the children had used movement while learning about the life cycle of plants (apples and pumpkins) and the water cycle, they were ready to create short movement performances in small groups. At the end of the unit, the children divided into groups and planned together how to demonstrate concepts about magnets.

Each group performed for the rest of the class, demonstrating one aspect of what they had learned. The performances included how some objects

181

Figure 8.4 Trini and Sarah dance their knowledge of magnets attracting and repelling.

attract and others do not, the north and south poles, and what it means to repel. Their favorite activity was to repel, spin around, and attract each other at weird angles. (See Figure 8.4.)

As each group performed, the rest of the class was the audience, and they had the job of interpreting the dance orally. The performers would tell them if they were correct. Later the children were thrilled to learn that siblings in fourth grade were also learning about magnets and had chosen tableaux as their way to demonstrate this learning.

Some ELLs are able to show what they know through movement, others through oral language or their writing or drawing. Because we give children opportunities to learn in a variety of ways, we also allow them to show what they have learned in a variety of ways. For example, during writing workshop or science workshop, children write nonfiction pieces about magnets or the water cycle. As they draw, label, and write their sentences we talk with the students, asking questions to clarify our understandings. Again, rubrics help teachers assess the learning.

Learning to Question and Wonder

Using magazines like *Your Big Backyard*, *Ranger Rick*, and *Zoo Animals*, we take time during science or reading workshop to teach children how to ask questions. After looking at a poster or pictures in a magazine, we record their questions. Often this is done in a small-group mini-lesson so all children will ask questions. Children learn how to ask different types of questions and how to find answers in a variety of ways. The following are questions children asked while looking at pictures in a magazine. They start simple and develop into more advanced "what if" questions. Emelie holds up a magazine and slowly turns the pages. She says, "I'm wondering which are the predators and which are the prey. What are you wondering?" As the children inch closer and closer to the magazine, they learn it is acceptable not to know everything. The questions start popping as the pages are turned.

"What is that?" "What is this?" "How many legs does it have?" "Why is the eagle eating the egg?" "Are those teeth?" "Does the bug die in his tummy or on his tongue?" "Can a frog eat a bird?" "It's not a crab. It's not a spider. What is it?" "What's this called?" "A bird can lay eggs in water?" "How long can a sloth hang upside down?" "How sticky is a chameleon's tongue?" "How does the light turn on in the lightening bug?" "This doesn't make sense. Why is a bald eagle called bald when he has feathers on his back?" "Why does an owl eat bunnies?" "Why does a snake take off his skin?" "Do birds shake snow off their heads?" "Why doesn't the butterfly freeze in the cold?" "Why does that bird live in a traffic light?" "Baby scared. Mommy gone?" "What if the lizards don't grow more tail?"

Children are learning that readers and scientists ask questions before, during, and after reading a book or participating in a unit of study. They are learning that there are many ways to find the answers and not everyone knows all the answers. These skills help them become better readers, problem-solvers, listeners, learners, and young scientists.

Science Learning Through Field Trips and Other Special Activities

Children find answers to their questions through books, investigations, experiments, structured play, and technology. However, we use many other methods for children to learn about the world around them.

Throughout the year, we plan field trips to enhance learning. We grapple with the question of timing. If we go at the beginning of the unit, it will certainly build schema. However, if we go near the end of the unit, students will have learned enough to have a deeper understanding of the experience. If we schedule the field trip somewhere in the middle of the unit, children have learned enough vocabulary, information, and processes to make connections.

Haider had learned a great deal about animals and their habitats before going to the petting zoo. The children were well prepared because we had studied many of the animals they would see. Haider had been involved in making Venn diagrams to compare animals, had drawn pictures of animals, and had labeled their habitats. He was especially fascinated with prairie dogs and their underground cities and had participated in making a prairie-dog habitat mural with a small group. He knew that even if there were no prairie dogs roaming, he could still find them. When he got tired of waiting to see a head pop up from a hole, he quickly climbed into the enclosure and peered into the opening of a mound before an adult could stop him.

We try to include as many parents on our field trips as we can. This exposes them to places they can take their families to on the weekend, as well as teaches them what their children are learning at school. For parents who speak limited English, we assign them children who speak their language. Thus, children will often engage in conversations on the trip in their home language.

Field trips are very popular with parents of ELLs. It is often a new experience for the adult to pet an ostrich or pick apples in an orchard. It also gives parents an opportunity to talk to their child about content learning. Feeding the goats or walking through the snake house nudges the parents into storytelling. Many students will come back to school the next day with "in my country" stories. Parents have told them stories about animals in Pakistan or milking cows on a farm in their home country.

Even though going in a school bus on a field trip is a major highlight of the year, we realize that there are many field trips we can take in our school and in our neighborhood to expand science learning. Each of our families signs "walking field trip" permission slips at the start of the year, allowing teachers to take their classes into the neighborhood at any time. In order for children to observe seasonal changes, teachers will take the same walking route many times during the year. "Looking for spring" walks occur weekly starting in March. Children learn to say goodbye to winter and look for signs of spring. Digital cameras snap pictures of the changes to post and write about later. We encourage parents to go with us and learn the importance of talking about daily changes and treasures in the world around us.

We take field trips into other classes to see displays, down hallways to learn from murals done by other classes, and to museums that classes have designed in our large open learning space. When we go on these mini field trips in the school, the students listen to other students share their learning.

As we walked upstairs to a third-grade museum named Continuity and Changes, student docents from Tricia Brown's class paired with younger students to stroll through the museum they had created. As each pair walked around, they stopped to play a learning game, examine posters, or touch artifacts. These one-on-one museum walks give children exposure to upper-grade curriculum presented in ways young children can understand. It gives

Figure 8.5 Erick listens attentively as Lester, his third-grade buddy, demonstrates how his simple machine works.

the children an opportunity to interact and have academic conversations with older children. (See Figure 8.5.)

At the end of our time in the exhibit hall, the third graders all sat eye-to-eye and knee-to-knee with younger students and reviewed what they had explored together. When we returned to our class, the students continued to talk, draw, and write about what we had learned.

At Bailey's our courtyard and garden areas provide for hands-on learning. The children prepare and plant in twelve small garden plots. The courtyard has plants native to Virginia, water and sand tables, and a pond, all of which can be used by small groups or the whole class for science learning. Children learn observational drawing to record the changes in plants over the seasons and to record other findings from walks.

Large, colorful painted murals are abundant in our hallways so that even while walking to lunch, children have opportunities to learn. Children work together on these murals as they are learning and add text to them. Children across grade levels as well as adults learn from the walls. Walking down the halls, a student can learn about the seasons, water cycles, life cycles, habitats, ants, crickets, or worms through reading the murals.

Field trips, touring child-generated museums, and "reading the halls" ensure that children are active learners engaged in science all day.

Inviting Parents to Be Partners in Science Learning

Newsletters and updates on class web sites keep the parents informed of the present unit of study. Teachers invite parents to come to the room and work side by side with their children or to share related artifacts or knowledge.

When the water-cycle video went home every night with a different child, the parents were thrilled. This taught the parents the science vocabulary the children were learning and enabled them to see their children working cooperatively and sharing their knowledge.

During the water-cycle unit, parents also received conversation-starter questions to help with getting children to tell more about their learning. Parents were told that if the question "What did you do today?" did not get a conversation going, they might want to try the following:

- Was the pond frozen today? Why?
- Did your class take the temperature outside today? Did the red go up or down?
- Why does it snow? (Help your child remember the words *ice crystals* and *water droplets*. They love to act out the ice crystals and water vapor sticking together, forming snow flakes, getting heavier and heavier, falling to the ground, and evaporating.)
- What happens to the snowflakes as they fall if the air is warm?
- Where does the snow go? Where does the ice go?
- What will happen if we put water outside tonight?

Besides encouraging parents to go on field trips and work in our rooms, we encourage them to study the walls and museums to learn about what their children are learning. The murals are visual representations of the learning going on in classes. Many of our neighborhood parents walk their children through the halls every morning to the classroom doors, and as children point out their contributions to murals, the parents become aware of new information and processes children are presently learning.

Parents are involved in creating and maintaining the courtyard space and garden area for science learning. They have shoveled, planted, and hauled stones and are very proud of the area. Often after school, parents and children wander through the area talking and observing.

By having conversations or making home visits, we know that the television is often on in many homes. We encourage families to watch the nature shows together. The children contribute a great deal to class discussions from what they have learned visually from those shows.

At family learning nights, it is heartwarming to see parents teach their children how to wire batteries to turn on a light or to see parents discussing findings under a microscope. Watching parents work side by side with children speaking their home language makes the work of putting these nights together worthwhile.

Emerging Scientists

We try to make science information understandable for children in many ways in stress-free environments where they can be confident young scientists: making connections, observing, gathering data, making conclusions, and sharing their learning with others.

At the end of the year, we can see how they have grown in their scientific thinking. Kindergarten and first-grade students spend recess time hunched over ant trails, leaning over plants in the garden, digging for worms, or gathering wisteria seeds. As they play at recess they continue their science questioning and learning on their own. Language is not getting in the way of these emerging scientists. They know that science learning goes on all day. The children are responding to their rich learning environment and the opportunities that teachers had provided.

We have one more story to share, this one about Eliza, who entered kindergarten in September from El Salvador as a preproductive English speaker. She grew from a bashful and silent little girl to a confident, English-speaking, wisecracking jokester.

Walking in from recess one day in May, the class read a sign that said to put trash in the can. As is our custom, two or three times a week we each pick up pieces of litter at recess and bring them into the school. Emelie called out over her shoulder, "Everyone grab three pieces of trash today." Emelie felt little arms go around her legs squeezing hard as Eliza tried to pick her up. Eliza giggled and yelled, "I've got my trash."

Students like Eliza and Oscar who proclaimed, "The words came down!" have flourished. They reaffirm our belief in teachers who strive to include English language learners as full and contributing members of their school communities. We applaud you!

REFERENCES

Professional Literature

Allington, Richard. 2001. *What Really Matters for Struggling Readers*. New York: Addison-Wesley.

Brady, Kathryn, Chip Wood, Deborah Portern, and Mary Beth Forton. 2003. *Rules in School*. Turners Falls, MA: Northeast Foundation for Children.

Calkins, Lucy. 2003. *Units of Study for Primary Writing: A Year-long Curriculum*. Teacher's College Reading and Writing Project. Portsmouth, NH: Heinemann.

Cambourne, Brian. 1988. *The Whole Story: Natural Learning and the Acquisition of Literacy in the Classroom*. New York: Ashton Scholastic.

Carpenter, Thomas P., Elizabeth Fennema, Megan Loef Franke, Linda Levi, and Susan Empson. 1999. *Children's Mathematics: Cognitively Guided Instruction*. Portsmouth, NH: Heinemann.

Chamot, Anna Uhl, and J. Michael O'Malley. 1994. *The CALLA Handbook: Implementing the Cognitive Academic Language Learning Approach*. New York: Addison-Wesley.

Clay, Marie, M. 1991. *Becoming Literate: The Construction of Inner Control*. Porstmouth, NH: Heinemann.

———. 1998. *By Different Paths to Common Outcomes*. Portland, ME: Stenhouse.

Collier, Virginia. 1995. *Promoting Academic Success for ESL Students*. Jersey City, NJ: New Jersey Teachers of English to Speakers of Other Languages/Bilingual Educators.

Collins, Kathy. 2004. *Growing Readers*. Portland, ME: Stenhouse.

Crowther, David T., and John Cannon. 2004. "Strategy Makeover: K-W-L to T-H-C." *Science and Children* (September): 42–44.

Cummings, Jim. 1979. "Cognitive/Academic Language Proficiency, Linguistic Interdependence, the Optimum Age Question and Some Other Matters." *Working Papers on Bilingualism* 19: 121–29.

———. 1996. *Negotiating Identity: Education for Empowerment in a Diverse Society*. Ontario, CA: California Association for Bilingual Education.

Fay, Kathleen, and Suzanne Whaley. 2005. "The Gift of Attention." *Educational Leadership* 62, 4: 76–79.

Fletcher, Ralph, and JoAnn Portalupi. 1998. *Craft Lessons: Teaching Writing K–8*. Portland, ME: Stenhouse.

Freeman, Yvonne, and David E. Freeman. 1992. *Whole Language for Second Language Learners*. Portsmouth, NH: Heinemann.

Horn, Martha. 2005. "Listening to Nysia: Storytelling as a Way into Writing in Kindergarten." *Language Arts* 83, 1: 33–41.

Johnston, Peter H. 2000. *Running Records: A Self-Tutoring Guide*. Portland, ME: Stenhouse.

Kinsella, Kate, and Kevin Feldman. 2003. *Narrowing the Language Gap: The Case for Explicit Vocabulary Instruction*. New York: Scholastic.

Kriete, Roxann. 2002. *The Morning Meeting Book*. Turners Falls, MA: Northeast Foundation for Children.

McCarrier, Andrea, Gay Su Pinnell, and Irene C. Fountas. 2000. *Interactive Writing: How Language and Literacy Come Together, K–2*. Portsmouth, NH: Heinemann.

Mere, Cathy. 2005. *More Than Guided Reading*. Portland, ME: Stenhouse.

Nelson, Jane. 1996. *Positive Discipline in the Classroom*. New York: Random House.

Payne, Carleen, and Mary Schulman. 1998. *Getting the Most Out of Morning Message and Other Shared Writing*. New York: Scholastic.

Peregoy, Suzanne F., and Owen F. Boyle. 1997. *Reading, Writing, & Learning in ESL*. White Plains, NY: Longman.

Reeves, Douglas R. 2005. "If I Said Something Wrong, I Was Afraid." *Educational Leadership* 62, 4: 72–74.

Richard-Amato, Patricia, and Marguerite Ann Snow. 1992. *Multicultural Classroom: Reading for Content-Area Teachers*. White Plains, NY: Longman.

Routman, Regie. 2003. *Reading Essentials: The Specifics You Need to Teach Reading Well*. Portsmouth, NH: Heinemann.

Samway, Katharine Davies, and Denise McKeon. 1999. *Myths and Realities: Best Practices for Language Minority Students*. Portsmouth, NH: Heinemann.

Tomilson, Carol Ann, and Jay McTighe. 2006. *Integrating Differentiated Instruction and Understanding by Design*. Alexandria, VA: Association for Supervision and Currriculum Development.

Vygotsky, Lev. 1978. *Mind in Society: The Development of Higher Psychological Processes*. Edited and translated M. Cole, V. John-Steiner, S. Scribner, and E. Souberman. Cambridge, MA: Harvard University Press.

———. 1986. *Thought and Language*. Rev. ed. Cambridge, MA: MIT Press.

Wiggins, Grant, and Jay McTighe. 2000. *Understanding by Design*. Alexandria, VA: Association for Supervision and Currriculum Development.

Zemelman, Steven, Harvey Daniels, and Arthur Hyde. 1993. *Best Practice New Standards for Teaching and Learning in America's Schools*. Portsmouth, NH: Heinemann.

Children's Books

Adler, David. 1989. *A Picture Book of Martin Luther King, Jr*. New York: Holiday House.

Baker, Jeannie. 2004. *Home*. New York: Greenwillow.

Bunting, Eve. 1994. *A Day's Work*. New York: Clarion.

Cannon, Janell. 1993. *Stellaluna*. New York: Harcourt.

Cherry, Lynn. 2000. *The Great Kapok Tree*. New York: Voyager.

Cowley, Joy. 1998. *Mrs. Wishy-Washy*. New York: McGraw-Hill.

Defoe, Daniel. 2003. *Robinson Crusoe*. New York: Penguin.

dePaola, Tomie, reteller. 1988. *The Legend of the Indian Paintbrush*. New York: G.P. Putnam's Sons.

Dufresne, Michele. 1998. *Emily's Babysitter*. Amherst, MA: Pioneer Valley Educational Press.

———. 2001. *Picking Apples*. Amherst, MA: Pioneer Valley Educational Press.

Fox, Mem. 1992. *Hattie and the Fox*. New York: Aladdin.

Franklin, Kristine. 1997. *Iguana Beach*. New York: Knopf.

Garland, Sherry. 1993. *The Lotus Seed*. New York: Harcourt.

George, Lindsay Barrett. 2004. *Inside Mouse, Outside Mouse*. New York: Greenwillow.

Goodall, John S. 1989. *The Story of a Farm*. New York: Margaret K. McElderry Books.

Hoffman, Mary. 2002. *The Color of Home*. New York: Dial.

Hunt, Roderick, and Alex Brychta. 2003. *Fetch*. Oxford, England: Oxford Reading Tree.

Hutchins, Pat. 1968. *Rosie's Walk*. New York: Simon & Schuster.

Johnston, Tony. 1991. *Yonder*. Staffordshire, England: Pied Piper.

———. 1998. *Amber on the Mountain*. New York: Penguin/Puffin.

Jorgensen, Gail. 1988. *Bubble Gum*. Orlando, FL: Rigby.

Karas, G. Brian. 2002. *Atlantic*. New York: G.P. Putnam's Sons.

Loretan, Sylvia, and Jan Lenica. 1991. *Bob the Snowman*. New York: Viking.

Munsch, Robert. 1995. *From Far Away*. Toronto, ON: Annick Press.

Murphy, Stuart J. 2002–2006. *Math Start* Series. New York: HarperCollins.

Myller, Rolf. 1991. *How Big Is a Foot?* New York: Yearling.

O'Neill, Alexis. 2002. *The Recess Queen*. New York: Scholastic.

Peek, Merle. 1985. *Mary Wore Her Red Dress and Henry Wore His Green Sneakers*. New York: Clarion.

Rylant, Cynthia. 1997. *Silver Packages*. New York: Scholastic.

Selsam, Millicent E. 1987. *Egg to Chick*. New York: Harper Trophy.

Shannon, David. 1999. *David Goes to School*. New York: Blue Sky Press.

Stanley, Diane. 1996. *Saving Sweetness*. New York: G.P. Putnam's Sons.

Stevens, Jan Romero. 1993. *Carlos and the Squash Plant*. Hong Kong: Northland Publishing.

———. 1995. *Carlos and the Cornfield*. Flagstaff, AZ: Rising Moon.

Waters, Kate. 1993. *Sarah Morton's Day*. New York: Scholastic.

———. 1996. *On the Mayflower*. New York: Scholastic.

———. 1996. *Samuel Eaton's Day*. New York: Scholastic.

———. 1996. *Tapenum's Day*. New York: Scholastic.

Wood, Audrey. 1985. *King Bidgood's in the Bathtub*. New York: Harcourt.

———. 1987. *Heckedy Peg*. New York: Harcourt.

Yashima, Taro. 1955. *Crow Boy*. New York: Viking.

Children's Magazines

Ranger Rick, *Your Big Backyard*, and *Zoo Animals*, all published by National Wildlife Federation.